Atla

and the

New

Consciousness

Stuart Wilson and Joanna Prentis

PO Box 754, Huntsville, AR 72740

800-935-0045 or 479-738-2348 fax 479-738-2448

www.ozarkmt.com

© 2011 by Stuart Wilson and Joanna Prentis

Second Printing - 2013

All rights reserved. No part of this book, in part or in whole, may be reproduced, transmitted or utilized in any form or by any means, electronic, photographic or mechanical, including photocopying, recording, or by any information storage and retrieval system without permission in writing from Ozark Mountain Publishing, Inc. except for brief quotations embodied in literary articles and reviews.

For permission, serialization, condensation, adaptions, or for our catalog of other publications, write to Ozark Mountain Publishing, Inc., P.O. Box 754, Huntsville, AR 72740, ATTN: Permissions Department.

Library of Congress Cataloging-in-Publication Data

Wilson, Stuart, 1937 -
Prentis, Joanna, 1943 -
    Atlantis and the New Consciousness, by Stuart Wilson and Joanna Prentis
A return to the Golden Era of Atlantis through hypnosis to understand how we can apply the lessons learned to the times now with the ascension process.

1. Atlantis   2. 2012   3. Ascension   4. Hypnosis   5. Metaphysics
I. Wilson, Stuart, 1937-   II. Prentis, Joanna, 1943-   III. Atlantis
IV. Metaphysics   IV. Title

Library of Congress Catalog Card Number: 2011928012
ISBN: 978-1-886940-20-8

Cover Art and Layout: www.noir33.com
Book set in: Times New Roman
Book Design: Julia Degan

Published by:

OZARK
MOUNTAIN
PUBLISHING

PO Box 754
Huntsville, AR 72740

WWW.OZARKMT.COM
Printed in the United States of America

Contents

Foreword:

The Starlight Centre

Beginnings

Joanna writes: It all began in 1988 when with my daughter, Tatanya, I set up the Starlight Centre in the West of England, a centre focusing on healing and the expansion of consciousness. Two years later, Stuart joined us to help with the development of the Centre, and he writes about this period:

It was inspiring and fascinating but also exhausting! A stream of visitors came in to the centre, mainly from the United States and Australia, but some also from Europe. We had an amazing and mind-expanding time sitting at the feet of internationally respected spiritual teachers and workshop leaders. What I remember most about this time was the big gatherings when our friends came in to share a meal and talk about our experiences and all the changes that were happening in our lives. It was a wonderful time, full of joy and laughter, and the special events - like Anna Mitchell Hedges sharing her crystal skull, a Magnified Healing workshop with Gisele King, and the two fire-walks led by Essassani - were simply magical!

Joanna: When I trained as a past life therapist with Ursula Markham, this gave the centre a new focus and a whole cycle of past life work began. Although we explored a number of historical periods, our work took a new direction through the gradual accumulation of seven past life subjects who had lives two thousand years ago in Israel. Most of these people were Essenes, and they told a remarkable story that ran parallel with the New Testament account but also contained some striking differences. Although it was not our intention at that time to write a book, the result of our work eventually produced enough material for a book called *The Essenes, Children of the Light,* which was published in March 2005 by Ozark Mountain Publishing in America.

Our pastlife work continued with subjects coming from the UK and from Spain and Germany, thanks to our friend Isabel Zaplana who proved to be a brilliant translator. And when seven subjects had completed their regressions, we had enough information for another book, which was published in 2009 as *Power of the Magdalene.*

We had already explored some past lives on Atlantis, the legendary ancient continent which was reputed to cover much of what is now the Atlantic ocean. And with the completion of our second book, Atlantis now became the main focus of our attention. But as always with pastlife work, little fragments from an earlier experience tend to weave their way into our present pattern, and we will begin this Atlantean story with something that happened back in 1993.

Part One:

Atlantis

1.

A Starship Crashes

Joanna comments: It all began with a past life session in February 1993 with a friend called Ken Driver. He had gone back to a life in Atlantis and I had asked him what his work was.

Ken: Teaching new ways from elsewhere. We came from Sirius but it was a mistake to come here. We were a scientific team, males and females. The females were more advanced.

But somebody wanted us to fail in our mission, someone back on Sirius. We weren't supposed to get back. They were sending us into exile, maybe even to our deaths, but we didn't know that. There was a problem with our ship. It crashed and most of our party were killed.

I could feel Ken's bafflement at why anyone would want to sabotage their ship. They were on a scientific mission, and he simply couldn't understand why they had been put at risk in that way. The incident was interesting, but didn't seem to lead on to any new information, so we simply put it aside as an isolated curiosity.

It was eleven years later in May 2004 when that the next piece of the jigsaw puzzle fell into place. I was doing a pastlife session with Stuart, and he was exploring a life he had never touched on before,

3

Stuart: We are getting ready for a journey: we are entering a starship. We are going with high hopes on a research mission and hope this will benefit both Sirius and the people of Atlantis.

Joanna: Are you from Sirius?

S: Yes.

J: What is your name?

S: I am called Anguel—there is a long 'A' sound at the beginning. (He spelled it out and pronounced it 'Aahn-quell.')

J: Are you a technician on Sirius?

Anquel: No, I am a counselor and an architect. It is my experience as an architect which has relevance for this mission. It is to be an exchange of knowledge and skills. Both governments will have to decide what is safe to exchange, so ours is an initial fact-finding mission to determine the extent and level of Atlantean skills, culture, and technology. We will tell the Atlanteans the broad areas of our technical expertise but will not reveal detailed technologies until our government has had a chance to review our report. It is hoped that both governments may gain from the final exchange because although our culture and technology is very advanced, there are some areas, particularly in the use of crystals, where Atlantis seems to be ahead of us.

J: Please move forward now in your experience. How does the journey turn out for you?

A: It does not go as we expected. It should have been routine, quite an easy and pleasant journey ... but there was some difficulty... the engine was faulty and we crashed upon a remote part of the Earth.

J: How far away from Atlantis did you crash?

A: Quite a distance. We crashed in a remote rocky area, very inhospitable.

J: *How many people were on the spacecraft?*

A: Eighteen, balanced nine and nine in the Sirian fashion, nine males and nine females.

J: *When you crashed how many survived?*

A: Four females and three males, but one male did not survive the journey.

J: *So you ended up with four females and two males?*

A: Yes. The male who survived only a short time was a great loss to us. He was one of the leading technicians on Sirius, and we were depending on him for the most complex technical analysis. He was badly injured in the crash and had internal bleeding. We had basic medical supplies and hand-held medical monitors but nothing that could address a serious problem of that nature.

Although he was injured, his mind was clear and under his direction we unbolted the casing around the engine. He was familiar with this pattern of engine and was able to identify quickly the component that was not part of the original design. Under his direction we removed this unit, and he examined it. He had expected it to be the crude production of some renegade terrorist and was surprised to find that it was efficiently designed and professionally constructed and bore all the signs of a piece of equipment coming from a government workshop. When he told us that, my heart sank for it had not occurred to me that our own government might be behind this crash.

The master technician explained to us the principle on which this device operated. A time clock set off the operation of the unit, which progressively throttled back the engine so that eventually no power at all would be available. Had it not been for the alertness and skill of our pilot in landing us quickly, we would all probably have been killed. The technician said that this was a device designed to ensure we crashed exactly where we did.

That made us all think furiously. As we argued it out, it became clear to us that if we had crashed on Atlantis, it might have caused a diplomatic incident with the Atlanteans blaming the Sirians for sending a defective starship which might endanger their citizens. Neither would it have served its purpose if the crash happened soon after take-off because then the engine might have been examined. And if we had stalled in space, we would simply have sent a signal back to Sirius, and we would have been rescued. No, it had to crash just before we got to Atlantis, and that was the most effective way of eliminating us. Our flight-plan would have been filed in advance in Central Records, and could have been accessed by anyone. From that plan it would have been comparatively easy to calculate the optimum time for arranging the crash.

When we realized this, we were all in shock. We had enemies we knew nothing about, and those enemies had abandoned us to our fate in this rocky landscape.

When we crashed, the structure of our starship was badly damaged, and some of the seats were torn from their anchor points. We had no digging tools and so we could not dig graves for our dead companions. And there were not enough rocks in that area to build a pile of stones over each body. What we did have was a full set of twelve flares which had survived the crash because they had been in a special box which was designed to withstand impact. We knew that the territory in which we had landed contained hostile and warlike tribes and for that reason judged it too dangerous to take the flares with us. They would have given light and long-lasting heat, but any fire at night might be seen from a distance and could attract the tribesmen. We were anxious about the possibility of being attacked in our sleep around a campfire, so we decided not to take the flares with us. Instead, we used them to cremate our dead colleagues.

We piled up the bodies in the middle of the ship and surrounded them with anything else that might burn. We lit the flares and moved away quickly. By then it was mid-afternoon, and we wished to put distance between us and the crash site before nightfall. We carried food and some essential equipment like the medical monitors—anything we could salvage from the crash.

One of the females was skilled in the use of the medical scanner and that showed the extent of the technician's injuries. We all had minor injuries, including cuts, bruises and one or two broken ribs, but his injuries were much more severe. Whenever we stopped we gave him healing under the direction of our leader. That held his condition static for a time but went no way towards curing it. Our basic medical kit, which had survived being well protected, could not begin to address his condition.

So we began to walk across this rocky and desolate landscape. The sun scorched us and the rain lashed us, and at night a cold wind blew. We found one or two caves along the way but mostly had to sleep in the open. The technician found the cold very difficult to bear. We are familiar with a technique for increasing the heat in the body, but he was so ill that he could not practice it. We all huddled around him to give him warmth but even so, when he awoke in the morning, his body felt like ice. We rubbed his limbs and gave him healing before we ate some rations and began the day's trek. He must have been in great pain, but he never complained. In my eyes he was a hero.

J: *Did you encounter any warlike tribesmen?*

A: We did our best to avoid them, hut our paths did cross a couple of times. The females were skilled in one technique which saved our lives: they cast what I can only call a net over the tribesmen's minds, so that their eyes ceased to see us and we vanished from the tribesmen's sight. The tribesmen must have assumed that we were ghosts, got frightened, and ran away.

J: *So did you get lost on your journey?*

A: No. We had maps in the starship which we took with us. We also had a little device which was able to pinpoint our position exactly. So we never got lost, but the journey was an extremely difficult one.

　　　The master-technician who had the internal bleeding got steadily weaker as we went along. Our treks grew shorter and our stops grew longer until at last he could go no further. He lay down on the rocky ground and we squatted down around him and held hands. We chanted for a while, and then, surrounded by his friends, he slipped away from us. There were many small rocks in that place, and we simply piled these on top of his body, said some sad words, and turned away. That was a bad day for us.

　　　After he died, we could not sleep that night, and as we huddled together, our leader, Solantha, broke down in tears and said she blamed herself for his death. I did my best to comfort her, saying that no one could have predicted the technical problems with our ship.

2.

Arrival in Atlantis

Anquel: When we finally reached the port, our luck changed. We found a ship which had come from Atlantis and was unloading its cargo and was due to sail back to Atlantis soon. I persuaded the captain that he would be rewarded by an official in Atlantis for carrying us free of charge, and he seemed satisfied with that. The sea journey took some days but it was calm, so we had a little time to recover from our ordeal.

On arrival on Atlantis, I made immediate contact with the official we were meant to be meeting and made sure the captain got his reward. We had advised the official of our time of departure from Sirius, but he had heard no other word from us and had become anxious. He had contacted Sirius, but they said they had not heard from us and started talking about the possibility of a crash somewhere on route. That made the official even more anxious, and so he was very glad to see us when we finally arrived. He proved both kind and efficient and looked after all our needs. He saw that we got excellent medical attention, good food, and fine quarters. He also provided counseling, as he realized we would all be in shock after such a terrible journey. And so we rested and began to recover.

Of course, our leader tried straight away to communicate with Sirius. The communication system, installed some time before by our own technicians, was audio only but of reasonably good quality. To use this system, it was necessary first to key in your personal code number. When our leader did so, there was a pause, and then she heard a recorded message saying:

The Sirian Scientific and Cultural Mission to Atlantis was destroyed in a tragic accident before it could reach its destination. All the participants in this mission are believed to have died when their starship crashed in a remote region with which we have no contact. This transmission ends.

Our leader told me at once of this development, and I tried to access the communication system by using my own code number. Again, there was a pause and the same recorded message. But this was soon followed by another recorded message:

This system is shutting down for routine maintenance.

That sounded ominous, and I was starting to feel confused.

Solantha called a meeting and updated the rest of our party on this new development. We were all in a state of shock about this. We had expected sympathy and support from the official on Sirius who had encouraged us to pursue this mission but instead it looked as if they were deliberately shutting down all communication with us.

Our leader proved a tower of strength at that point. She said that without official backing, there was no point in continuing with the mission. We might get some clarification when communications with Sirus were restored or some Sirian diplomat arrived, but until then, we were free to pursue our own course of action.

I began to suspect that the situation had become more complex when the communication system was not reinstated during the next six months, and it was another five months before we got any news at all from Sirius. This came quite by chance from a Sirian academic who had traveled via another star system. He happened to encounter our leader when walking through one of the squares in the city, and he recognized her at once. Solantha told me his face went white when he saw her. She talked briefly with him and then gathered our group together. We all settled down in the rather luxurious visitor accommodation that had been allocated to him. First, our leader gave a brief summary of the fate of our mission, and then the academic spoke.

"First of all," he said, "I want to say how much I sympathize with you. From what Solantha has said, it's clear you've been through a terrible ordeal." He paused and gave a sigh. "The news of your accident was a shock for all of us in the academic community, and the Council made it clear that as your starship had come down in a very remote and hostile area there was no possibility of getting any further information on the cause of the crash. Frankly, my suspicions were aroused from the start. That model of starship had been in service for years, and there had never been any kind of problem with it, let alone a fatal crash. It sounded all too convenient that we would never be able to tell what really happened, and I suspected a political cover-up.

"I made enquiries amongst some old friends who know how the political system works, and through them I discovered that the prospect of an exchange mission had aroused powerful opposition. It was not so much the exchange of cultural information but the exchange of technology that had proved so alarming. The opposing view was that some of this technology, if it fell into the wrong hands, might threaten the future defense and security of Sirius. Apparently, there had been a good deal of argument about this behind the scenes, although it never became official policy to stop your mission. I think it's most likely that some over-zealous security operatives decided that you must be stopped, and they acted without authorization.

"Once you became seriously overdue, it was concluded that you must have crashed and some sort of inquiry must have been carried out. If it was discovered that these operatives had acted on their own initiative, the Council might have been overcome with embarrassment. No government likes to admit that its security people can get out of control. Rather than identify the problem to the Atlanteans, the Council might have preferred to label this as a tragic accident, hoping that you would never surface to challenge that story.

"I'm afraid you're all officially dead, and it would probably be wise for you to maintain that fiction. If the security people behind all this are still at large, it would be much too dangerous for you to try to return since they might be ruthless in covering their tracks.

"Of course I can secretly convey any messages you may have to relatives or friends, but I think that's all that can be done in the circumstances. Frankly, I think you've been treated outrageously, but I honestly don't see what else can be done."

There was a long silence after he had finished speaking, and it took us some while to take it all in. I had believed our mission had official backing to the highest level, but in reality it had been controversial and had aroused fierce opposition.

When I heard this account of events I began to understand the whole thing clearly for the first time. Now our difficulties in contacting Sirius all made perfect sense to me. I saw then that there was to be no going back for any of us. We had better accept our exile and get on with our lives here as best we could.

J: *How did the rest of your party take this news?*

12

A: We were all in shock. No one likes to have permanent exile from their homeland forced upon them, especially if they think they are carrying out the wishes of their government. There was bitterness and resentment in the group, but we received expert counseling, and in time we were able to release these feelings and move on.

3.

The Atlantean Experience

We wondered how Anquel's party would settle down on Atlantis after so traumatic a journey, and when we questioned him about it, this was his response:

Anquel: Looking back, I saw that the meeting with the academic was a turning point for us. It helped us to put the whole dreadful experience of the crash and the nightmare journey behind us. By the time the academic arrived, we had already begun to pick up the threads of our lives, and all of us had found work of some kind.

Joanna: And did you all manage to find work that suited you?

A: Our education, knowledge, and, in some cases, technical skills were in advance of those on Atlantis, so all of us managed to find interesting work. Our leader became a senior lecturer at the leading university, and later a much-honored Head of Science at that university. I studied architecture for about six months, mainly to familiarize myself with what materials were available, some of which were quite different from those on Sirius. I then set up my own practice, became quite successful, and built a good life for myself. I think my clients liked to deal with such an exotic creature as a Sirian because long-stay visitors from other star systems were still quite rare. In time all of us settled down and adopted Atlantis as our home, but we never forgot our strange and painful arrival on this planet.

J: *What sort of buildings did you work on as an architect?*

A: Mainly houses and spaces for therapy. I became quite skilled in providing exactly the right space for various therapies in terms of the sound and light input, embedding crystals in the structure and using advanced geometrics. On Sirius it was all much more advanced and there was almost an architectural manual for every kind of building, but in Atlantis we were much more free to experiment. Sometimes the free experimentation, especially by technologists pursuing some scientific theory, went too far, and I felt we would have been more careful on Sirius, but I did enjoy the freedom to develop in any way that seemed interesting and fruitful.

J: *And you were able to study Atlantean culture which must have been quite different from that on Sirius.*

A: Indeed, but you must bear in mind that Sirian culture was much older, and some things about Atlantean culture were familiar to us from similar periods in our own development. Taken as a whole, I found Atlantean culture most interesting. The main division by occupation was quite different to that used on Sirius. The Atlanteans had four main occupational groups:

Those Who Seek Exact Knowledge. This group included the scientists and technologists.

Those Who Attune to Sacred Energies. This group included the seers and priests.

Those Who Construct Perfect Relationships. This included the architects and builders. Architecture encompasses the relationship of different parts of a building to each other, the relationship of people to the building as a whole, and the relationship of the building to the surrounding landscape.

Those Who Facilitate Balance and Harmony. This included counselors and therapists.

J: *And did you find Atlantean society as a whole very different to the society you were used to on Sirius?*

A: Yes. Sirian culture is highly structured and organized and leaves less room for individual creative experimentation than some might wish. At first I saw the openness, the willingness to engage in experiment and open-ended enquiry, as one of the great strengths of Atlantean civilization. But later, when I had spent some years there, I began to become uneasy about where all this experimenting might lead to.

I knew, for example, that some of the experiments based upon sound were having very damaging side-effects. Sound is regarded with respect in most advanced star-systems, and we knew its power. I felt that the Atlanteans should have consulted other civilizations who had already developed sound and not simply gone at break-neck speed into experimenting without first considering the possible dangers.

J: *How did you keep yourself fit?*

A: I exercised daily with a slow meditational form of movement which was popular amongst the Atlanteans, and I used to walk as often as I could through the many parks and open spaces in the city.

J: *Was the communication system ever opened up again?*

A: Not in my lifetime, nor did I notice any visiting official from Sirius, but then I didn't expect to. I had put the Sirian part of my life behind me and had become accustomed to the Atlantean ways. Our group continued to meet for a time, yet in the end,even these meetings ceased for none of us wished to prolong the painful memories of the past. But I remained close to Solantha and watched her rise in the Atlantean academic world with some pride and satisfaction.

J: *How would you sum up the Atlantean civilization?*

A: I found the openness, the willingness to experiment and find new ways of doing things, one of the chief attractions of the Atlantean temperament. In comparison the culture of Sirius, being much older, had had time to settle down, become highly structured and perhaps a little set in its ways. But over the years, I came to see also a more troubling aspect to Atlantis. The constant drive to develop new and creative technologies had its dark side, and I saw some people being hurt in this rush towards all things new. And out of the technology side of this society came even darker forces, an impulse to manipulate people, and a drive towards power and control. I saw some people who had gone down that road so far that they had closed their hearts and become hard like the machines they worked with. There were many kind and helpful people on Atlantis, and I had the good fortune to meet quite a number of them, but I saw those other ones, too.

4.

The Design of Atlantean Cities

There was one aspect of Anquel's life we wanted to follow up, so we asked him about this during a later session:

Joanna: You mentioned designing houses: Were these in villages or in cities?

Anquel: They were all in cities. When I started to get commissions for houses, I spent some time doing a survey of the most architecturally interesting cities in Atlantis. I found them highly original and creative, and there were many popular designs including some based on pyramids, rectangles and curves.

1. Designs based on the pyramid form. Several cities had all their buildings shaped like pyramids but in a very creative way with a mixture of large and small pyramids, some seeming to merge into the buildings closest to them so that it was a rolling landscape of pyramidal structures, connected by a series of walkways. I must admit when I first saw a city built on these lines, I was astonished, for the sheer exuberance of it quite took my breath away. Yes, they used pyramid forms on Sirius, but these were always separate and self-contained. To merge different sizes of pyramids was something much bolder than I had ever seen. All this pyramidal creativity was very stimulating from the

visual standpoint, and I could see why people would want to live there.

2. Square or rectangular buildings were also popular, of course, but it was the placing of doors and windows that made all the difference. In one city I visited, this placing was perfectly judged with the eye flowing easily over a series of harmonious resonances and being led naturally from one window or door to the next. Taking in these perfect proportions was like listening to some cool and contrapuntal music that suggested perfect harmony.

3. The opposite to a rectangular approach was one city I visited where all the surfaces were curved. The windows were round or oval, and the door units were oval in shape with a pair of doors in the middle. The colors chosen were all shades of brown from the palest buff to a rich dark brown. These brown hues combined with a mass of curves to give a very pleasant overall effect with the buildings flowing together in a very attractive manner.

4. The most extreme use of color that I saw involved great slabs of color, for example, a large wall in a bright pink or a rich yellow. Here the walls became powerful color statements in their own right, a bold approach but not one that everyone might be happy with.

5. Then there were the "garden cities" where all the buildings were set within parks and gardens. Some of these cities were more successful than others, and I concluded that there needed to be a good variety in the design and planting of these gardens for this format to work.

6. I remember one city where all the buildings looked like temples. The ones that really were temples were larger, of course, and had more space around them, but every single house in the city was like a miniature temple, complete with columns. I'm not sure this was really a very good idea—one went away from that location feeling somewhat "over-templed."

7. I have left one of the most striking designs to the last. Imagine a cluster of houses, all with six sides like cells in a honeycomb. They are grouped together so that they have linking walls, and in the middle of this cluster of six houses there is a garden. Now think of that cluster of six houses as one cell and imagine larger cell groupings—cells within cells aggregating until they form a city with thousands of houses. In every case there are six units clustered around a central space: a garden for the six houses, and either large gardens or parks for the larger spaces. The big advantage of this design was that because the six houses were linked with shared walls that made them very strong and earthquake resistant. The central gardens were also a popular feature. They were enclosed and private, a good place for the children to play. And as large glazed doors from each of the houses led directly onto the garden, it was the ideal place to meet and talk with your neighbors. This building format was particularly popular with groups of friends with similar interests—families of musicians, or artists or counselors and so on. Six of these families would choose to live around the shared garden, and I could see the advantage of living close to your friends. The only disadvantage of this design was that some of the rooms in these houses had very strange shapes!

J: *Surely a city with all the houses looking the same would be a place where you could easily become lost.*

A: That's exactly what I thought when I first heard of this design, but I found they had solved this problem in a very ingenious way. In the six main blocks making up a city, they had painted all the front doors in bold colors—red, blue, yellow, green, orange, and violet. These colors followed each other clockwise in spectrum order, and everyone knew where these colors fitted in the overall map of the city. So simply by looking at a door, you could tell at once which sector of the city you were in, and how that sector was related to other areas—how the blue sector related to orange sector, for example.

They also painted the doors of the outside houses within each sector in the strongest color, paling in hue as you moved into the middle of the sector, so at a glance you also knew how near the center of the sector you were, just by looking at the nearest front door. I had never seen color-coding used in this way before, and it struck me as very ingenious.

What I particularly enjoyed upon Atlantis was the great sense of creative freedom, something that just didn't exist to the same degree on Sirius, which was an older civilization with more rules and structures in it. On Atlantis you could let your imagination take flight and come up with any creative idea, however daring. Some of these ideas were failures, of course, but we had great fun putting the successes into practice, and this free environment seemed to bring out the best in everyone. Nobody felt tied down by any kind of rigid or oppressive system, and that helped people to relax and give of their very best.

5.

Zaritha

We had followed Anquel for some time as he arrived on Atlantis and began to establish himself there, but one question still remained to be answered.

J: *You said that in time all of your group settled down on Atlantis. Did you get married?*

A: Yes, but not at once. I had not married back on Sirius because I was still establishing myself in my career. And at first on Atlantis, I had a lot of adjustment to do within the architectural world—it was almost like being a student again.

    Once I set up my own practice, success came quickly, and then I relaxed, and I suppose I became more open to new possibilities in my life.

    I had many friends amongst the Atlantean community of architects, and I met my future wife at a dinner party given by one of these friends. He told me before the party that she was the widow of a brilliant young scientist who had died in a tragic laboratory accident.

J: *Was that kind of accident unusual?*

A: Sadly, no. They were all too common at that time. The Atlantean safety standards were notoriously inadequate. For them it was exploration and discovery at any price—but we Sirians knew that research can be a dangerous business. When you're just beginning to understand some new area of science, you can't see all the possible benefits, but you can't see the dangers either.

J: *So this young widow, what was her name?*

A: She was called Zaritha. (He pronounced this as Zahreetha.) She had fair hair and magical blue eyes. We became friends at once, enjoyed each other's company, shared the same sense of humor and were married within a year. By then I was 36 and she was 27.

Her intelligence—and sheer common sense—saved me from going down many a professional blind alley, and as we grew together, I came to value her more and more. We were not blessed with children, but in every other way it was a perfect marriage.

Zaritha was able to fill in the many gaps in my knowledge of Atlantean society, and as she worked as a counselor in one of the temples, I came to understand their mode of therapy, too. I concluded that counseling on Sirius—which was held in high regard throughout our galaxy—was, taken as a whole, in advance of Atlantean practice, but I came to understand that the Atlantean ability to blend their mind-therapy with the deep spiritual side of their nature gave it a strength and profound meaningfulness that Sirian counseling lacked. Their ability to use simple ceremonies in a temple setting to mark stages in the progress of the therapy was also exemplary, and the larger ceremonies marking rites of passage—from child to young person, from young person to adult, for example—could be seen as potent tools binding their society together. I saw that they gave the individual the public recognition he/she needed—an acknowledgment that he/she had moved into a different phase of his/her life. And I realized that if this recognition is not given, the process of-moving on can be undermined and much distress felt by the individual because his/her new status and extended role in society is not acknowledged.

Once we were married, we got into the full swing of the Atlantean dinner party process, which on the whole I enjoyed. This was a wonderful way of meeting new friends, and if I am honest, I did make a lot of good business contacts that way as well. However, it did bring out sharply the difference between Sirian and Atlantean culture, especially in the case of one dinner party that I remember.

Later in the evenings, when the children were safely in bed, these parties moved up into a different gear. Back on Sirius, sexual practices were considered as something to be kept strictly between the two people concerned, and perhaps also their counselor if they were encountering some problems. It's not that we were prudish about these things, but Sirian society has a very highly developed sense of tact and delicacy. Yet in these late evening parties on Atlantis, I found that many of the guests seemed to talk quite freely about these matters. The best sexual positions, the most extreme and ecstatic sensations—everything seemed to be discussed quite openly and with no apparent embarrassment. And in this one particular dinner party, the whole thing was brought into sharp focus for me.

It was a party of more mature people in their thirties and forties, but about a third of the guests were much younger, in their mid-twenties. As we lingered over our wine at the long dinner table a young couple were trying to describe a very obscure and gymnastic sexual position—something that many of the older ones, including myself, had difficulty visualizing. Eventually the young man grew impatient, "Oh, don't worry," he said, "'we'll demonstrate it for you!"

So the long dining table was cleared, flat cushions were laid out on it, and the young couple went into their gymnastic demonstration with great gusto. My wife, knowing how different Sirian culture was to her own, realized that this sort of thing would be most embarrassing for me, so she held my hand tightly under the table until the young couple finished to delighted shouts and vigorous applause.

On Sirius that kind of demonstration would have been greeted by a stony silence of acute embarrassment, and from that point on, the couple would have been shunned by most of Sirian society. I did wonder-whether this couple would become outcasts, too, and said as much to my wife on our journey home. In response I remember she just laughed and said, "Well, let's wait and see."

But as it turned out, Zatitha knew her fellow Atlanteans much better than I did. The young couple became instant celebrities, and many other dinner parties wanted to stage a repeat performance.

Then I saw clearly for the first time that I had landed in a very strange and alien place, indeed—somewhere totally different from my Sirian origins. Yes, I was still committed to staying on Atlantis and making a life there because going back to Sirius was quite impossible. But I think from that day on, I became more wary of excesses of all kinds in Atlantean society although I was wise enough to keep my thoughts to myself and confide in no one—not even my beloved Zaritha.

Comment by Stuart: This chapter, more than any other, brings home the difference between Sirian and Atlantean society. This one episode of the dinner party is like a dramatization of Atlantis on a miniature scale. Here you can sense the tension between restraint and excess, a tension that spilled over into a major split in Atlantean society. And there is a hint, too, of the forces that had already destroyed earlier periods of Atlantean civilization—a theme we will return to later in this book.

Part Two:

Alariel

6.

First Meeting with Alariel

We have been writing these books very much on the basis of our inner guidance and have learned to trust that guidance over the years. And there was one instance when our guidance helped us to open a door to greater knowledge that would otherwise have been closed to us. Stuart's life as Anquel had already provided a good deal of interesting information, but we were surprised and excited when our guidance told us that Anquel also had access to a much more profound and significant source. And we were told that our best chance of accessing this source would be to ask Anquel a question which we knew he would be unable to answer.

This began a process of casting about for a suitable question to ask. We already knew that Anquel had an interest in a "slow meditational form of movement" and this sounded to us something like an Atlantean form of Tai Chi. Taking this as our starting point, we then constructed a question along the lines that our guidance had suggested and put this question to Anquel.

Joanna: We are interested in the slow meditational form of movement which you mentioned. There is a group of people called the Essenes who live many thousands of years in the future from your time. We understand that the Essenes have a form of meditational movement and wonder if you could research this for us.

Anquel: I have never heard of these people, and, if they exist in the future I would have no way of researching this information by conventional means. However, I do have an angelic source who might be able to help; I will ask him to speak to you directly.

There followed a long pause, and I had the sense of a different energy begin to focus through Stuart. Then the communication began again:

This is Alariel, speaking for a group of twelve angels who work with the Order of Melchizedek. We understand you have a question concerning the Essenes, a Brotherhood which is known to us.

Joanna: Thank you, Alariel. Yes, we would like to know if the Essenes practiced a kind of slow meditational form of movement.

Alariel: Yes, but only in the northern group of communities. There were seven sequences of movement, each having a symbolic significance:

Earth, represented by the lion,
Water, represented by the fish,
Fire, represented by the dragon,
Air, represented by the dove,
Body, represented by the bear,
Mind, represented by the wolf,
Spirit, represented by the eagle.

The movement of all these creatures was imitated in the sequences, and the whole form gave the sense of gathering all of creation into one unified flow of energy. This form came out of the work of a group of Essenes who lived at Mount Carmel. The accommodation there was more confined than that experienced at the larger communities which covered a greater area of land, and there was a need to develop a system which would exercise the body in a small space. So it was that special need that gave rise to this form, and it did spread to some other communities in the northern group, but it was not widely practiced.

J: *Thank you, Alariel that is most interesting. You say that you speak for a group of angels. Is there anything else about yourself that you would like to tell us? Your position in the angelic world, for example?*

A: We work as a group and do not focus on the personal level. In the angelic world, it is the work that is important, not the individual angel.

J: *Could you please tell us some more about your group, then?*

A: The members of our group have worked with the Melchizedek Order on a number of planetary systems over a long period of time. It is our joy and privilege to work with the Melchizedeks because they are so focused on the Light. Since we became specialized in our work, it was considered appropriate that we should dialogue with groups such as your own, who have an interest in the work of the Order.

J: *Are there any limits to these dialogues that you can foresee?*

A: These communications will be limited more by your ability to conceive and phrase questions than by our ability to answer them. We respond to what is asked, and if you don't ask specific questions, you are likely to get only general answers. The more specific the questions are, the more they will bring forth information on the things you are interested in. As these dialogues continue, you may find the quality of the questions increases and so more interesting answers will emerge. The Universe is vast, and there are some areas of knowledge that go beyond our experience, but much remains for you to explore.

J: *Well, thank you for this chance to dialogue with you: we shall try to come up with some good questions. And are there any questions you are forbidden to answer?*

A: There are some questions that we *choose* not to answer, and these come into three categories:

1) There are Words of Power which give access to control frequencies in the angelic world. We obviously would not reveal these.

2) There is information which forms part of the research which other groups on Earth are well advanced on and will soon reveal—we would not wish to "steal their thunder."

3) And finally there are concepts so far beyond your present understanding that they would disorient you and cause you distress; it is not a kindness to reveal this type of information, and we will not do so.

Having said that, there is still a vast amount of information for you to explore.

J: *We appreciate that these communications are a great opportunity: why has this opportunity been given to us?*

A: When you sent your first book out into the world, it opened up a doorway of Light, a portal leading to future possibilities. These dialogues are one of the results of opening that doorway. The reward of work is more work, but it gets more interesting as your consciousness develops!

Our relationship with Alariel changed and evolved over the next few months, and, gradually through this contact, we came to see him as a source of remarkable depth and clarity. Some of the information we received surprised us, and much of it stretched our imagination and challenged us to expand our awareness.

Over a period of time, our dialogues with Alariel began to transform our work, and his insight and knowledge gave our research a depth which a pastlife process alone could not have provided. This was clearly a most useful resource, and it was enabling us to probe areas that had so far proved elusive. Where there were gaps in the past life record, we could use Alariel's knowledge to fill these in and obtain a more complete picture. For example, we had not been able to identify the date of Anquel's arrival on Atlantis until we asked Alariel about this.

A: Anquel and his companions came to Atlantis in 25,000 BCE. This was at a time when Atlantis had been reseeded again with incoming souls. It was well before the Golden Age, which began around 14,000 BCE.

Comment by Stuart: Throughout this book, we have used the modern equivalents CE (Common Era) and BCE (Before the Common Era) rather than the traditional terms BC and AD, as the latter is represented by many non-Christian groups.

Part Three:

Golden Atlantis

7.

The Village and the City

Anquel had painted a fascinating picture of Atlantis, and he saw it with the eye of a detached observer. He described an organized, structured, intellectual, and scientific culture, but there was little sense of a high level of spirituality or the use of consciousness in esoteric and subtle ways. And in his summing up of Atlantean civilization, he hinted at something much darker. All this helps us to put him into some kind of perspective within the arc of Atlantean civilization.

Taken as a whole, Anquel's story does not sound like an account of Golden Atlantis, the relatively short high peak of Atlantean civilization which occurred toward the end of the whole cycle; it sounds much more like an earlier period, perhaps at the beginning of a stage when it had not degenerated into selfishness and conflict. The seeds of that conflict were clearly visible to Anquel, but the society had not yet fully polarized into opposing camps in his day.

Our assessment that Anquel's group had come to Atlantis well before the Golden Age was confirmed by reading Diana Cooper's fascinating book, *Discover Atlantis,* written with Shaaron Hutton. The dating of Atlantis remains uncertain with wide divergences of opinion between authors, but a possible dating of the Golden Era might be between 14,000 and 12,500 BCE. When we came to investigate Atlantis, we thought we would begin by trying to get some clarification on the chronology.

Joanna: Various authors talk about Golden Atlantis lasting for different periods of time. Some say about ten thousand years and some only 1500 years. How do you perceive this?

Alariel: It was always going to be difficult to sustain a civilization at a very high vibrational level. You could achieve it if you vetted all those coming in to be born and excluded all those of lower vibration, only allowing in the souls with the very highest and purest consciousness. As Atlantis was considered to be a school of spiritual evolution for a wide range of beings, the input was never controlled that rigidly.

It was hoped that with a majority of high vibrational people in place, they would inspire the incoming souls to higher achievement than they had managed in their previous lives elsewhere.

Sadly that was not the continuing pattern during any of the five main epochs of Atlantean development, and each epoch became volatile and difficult to sustain. That is why the 1500 year period of time is the correct one as those conditions were so hard to keep in a stable and enduring balance for long periods of time. Keeping Atlantis going at the Golden Peak level even for 1500 years was a major achievement from our point of view.

Continued success in sustaining this high vibrational level could only have been achieved with a much tighter control of who was born there, and that was, in our view, wisely considered not to be desirable. Atlantis was never set up as a cozy "club" for beings of elevated vibration only. It was designed as a school for spiritual evolution in which beings at a number of levels would be able to learn and develop with the ones of higher consciousness leading and inspiring the rest.

In that framework there was always the danger that the primitive ones would fail to understand and value the advanced ones and move against them using violent methods that the higher ones would not stoop to employ. This happened again and again, but it did not mean that the basic philosophy behind the Atlantean experiment was mistaken or deeply flawed. Each time an Atlantean epoch was set up, human consciousness moved onwards towards the Light, and the final flowering of that consciousness during Golden Atlantis has resonances right up to the present day. Humanity needs all its triumphs if it is to focus on what can be achieved and if it is to be inspired in its journey to the Light.

Comment by Stuart: Alariel gives more information on Atlantean chronology in the chapter called "The Five Phases of Atlantis."

Golden Atlantis certainly does sound wonderful and inspiring. This period has such relevance today as we aspire to live in lighter and more positive ways, and we wanted to access information on it for ourselves. When Stuart was regressed to a life in this period, this is how the session began.

J: *Please describe what you are seeing.*

Stuart: I am walking up a gentle slope toward a temple. It is pyramid-shaped and built of polished green stone.

J: *And what is your name?*

Stuart: I am called Sykla. *(He pronounced this name as 'See-kla.' Now that Sykla has identified himself, we will use that name.)*

J: *So you are going up towards this temple.*

Sykla: Yes. Inside this temple is not elaborate, just white walls, and there's a simple stone altar with one crystal, a beautiful purple-colored crystal.

J: *Is it a single point or a cluster?*
S: It's one large point. This is a place of realignment where people come to have their energy fields realigned. This we do regularly to keep ourselves in good health.

As I look out from the entrance to the temple, the land slopes away and there is water which looks almost like a river, but it's man-made. This water is surrounding the temple.

J: *Tell me about this healing process in the temple.*
S: The Priestess, who is called Aneetha, conducts the healing. You lie on a couch and the Priestess goes round with an orange-colored crystal which she holds in her hands—it's quite a deep orange, fading off into golden yellow. She uses this to cleanse the chakras and realign the energy.

J: *Are you talking about seven chakras here?*
S: This is a twelve chakra system, eight in the body, one below and three more above. Twelve is a key number for us.

Comment by Stuart: In addition to the seven widely accepted chakras, the 12-chakra system used on Atlantis also included these five chakras:
1. Stellar Gateway – two hand's lengths above the head;
2. Soul Star – one hand's length above the head;
3. Causal chakra – a hand's width behind the back of the head;
4. Navel chakra – at the navel;
5. Earth Star – one hand's length below the feet.

Readers who wish to read more about the 12-chakra system of Atlantis are advised to read the most authoritative source: Chapter 16, "The Chakras of Atlantis" in *Discover Atlantis* by Diana Cooper and Shaaron Hutton (see Further Reading reference under Cooper.)

J: *The central crystal—you said it was a big purple crystal. Maybe an amethyst? How big is it?*

S: If I put my arms around it, my hands wouldn't meet.

J: *Oh, **really** large. And what does this big crystal do?*

S: It supplies energy in some way, but the actual direction of the healing, the way the chakras are aligned, and the other lines in the body are all connected up. Because she works on three lines going down the body, all of that is fine-tuned by the crystal in her hands. So the power is supplied by the big crystal, and the fine-tuning and the direction of the power is provided by the small crystal—they are linked in some way, but I don't understand exactly how.

Comment by Stuart: This sounds as if the priestess might have been using the Axiatonal maintenance lines. The existence of these lines was first described by J.J. Hurtak in *The Keys of Enoch*. This book is considered a classic text, a unique source-book on esoteric knowledge. The section on Axiatonal lines (Key 3-1-7) describes the use of the basic energy of the universe in order to grow new tissue and even new limbs. It talks about the merging of molecular biology and medical astronomy (see *Keys of Enoch* page 521 and the Further Reading reference under Hurtak.)

    While the full development of medical systems based on the Axiatonal energy grid (also called the Cosmic Lattice) is still some way into the future, it may be noted that various therapy systems based on Axiatonal energy have already been developed. The therapies—under names like Axiatonal Alignment Therapy, Galaxial Infusion and Reconnective Healing—are based on reconnecting the individual with the universal energy grid. The first report of these new therapies was the article, "Axiatonal Therapy"—an interview with Janet DiGiovanna which appeared in *Body Mind Spirit* in August 1995.

A remarkable painting of this energy system can be found in *Sacred Mirrors* by Alex Grey.

The session continues.

J: *And she's using the crystal off-body?*
S: Yes, just above the body. This kind of treatment is a regular thing for us.
J: *When you say "regular," do you mean once a week?*
S: No, once a month. It's a maintainer of good health rather than a solver of problems.
J: *And she's just using crystals, she's not working with sound or color?*
S: No. She has chosen to work in silence, just using the crystals. But apparently you can do this alignment in a number of ways, depending on your training.

So I feel very good as I come out of the temple with my energy all balanced. And there's a slight slope going down from the temple, and then there's the water. I take a small boat to cross the water, and then there are some round houses, set in little groups. I live in the next area beyond another stretch of water. When I reach that point, I see a number of people going about their usual work growing crops or making pottery. But we also work together sometimes. When houses are made, we all come together to help in doing this.

On very special days we go to the big temple at the center of our region by taking transporters that are powered by crystals. We come to this big temple, and there is a reconnection for everyone. The High Priest there is very powerful. You don't know very much about what these High Priests and High Priestesses do. They are mysterious beings. They seem to have access to knowledge in a more direct way than we do. And they know our connections to the stars much more than we do and more about the history of our people.

J: *And what work do you do?*

S: I help in the making of buildings.

J: *Did you help in building the temple?*

S: The small temple in our area, yes, but not the big temple for the whole region. That is much older.

J: *Do you know the name of the big temple?*

S: The Temple of Zoltha, and that is linked to the sun and to the lion people. There are images of lions in the temple that have something to do with the source of the original founder of this temple.

J: *So could you tell us more about your work?*

S: The siting of a house in the landscape is important. The Earth tells us where she would wish the house to be. I have a skill in tuning in to where the house should be in relation to the landscape. The houses need to sit well in the landscape and be accepted by it, become part of it.

J: *Do you have a guardian of the Earth you tune into?*

S: I attune to the landscape and the angel of the landscape to find out where the house should be. And when you look at these houses after they have been there for some time, they look as if they have grown out of the landscape.

Comment by Stuart: This section is fascinating because there are parallels here with Feng Shui. It seems that the Chinese art of geomancy, which included the "auspicious" placing of buildings, might have its roots in a much more ancient practice which flourished on Atlantis. Feng Shui is the Chinese art of locating or creating fortunate places in which to live and work. It is based upon co-operating and harmonizing with the localized energy currents of chi or cosmic energy.

The session continues.

J: *Is the land around where you live low-lying?*

S: The temple is on the highest part of the land, and it slopes away from the temple in a series of strips of land, like rings with water between the rings in concentric circles. All the rings being centered on the temple. And far away below down there is a river.

J: *Where are you going on this day after your rebalancing at the temple?*

S: I'm going to my house, the place where I work. I'm working at the moment on a meeting house because in this area a larger one is needed now. When the sun goes down, everyone goes back to their own houses, but sometimes we visit friends and go to their house to have an evening meal with them.

J: *What do the houses in your village look like?*

S: As a community we chose a traditional style of building, houses in wood and stone with thatched roofs. We felt this would help our village to blend into the landscape and integrate with nature. People in the cities may choose different patterns of building, some using advanced geometry and the contrast of big areas of glass and stone, but that would be too elaborate for us—we wanted a simple and natural effect.

J: *How do you light and heat your houses?*

S: The lighting is provided by crystals, which are designed to glow with various degrees of intensity. We heat our houses with units that capture the sun's energy and intensify it through a crystal grid, and we use a similar system for cooking.

J: *You mentioned a meeting hall. What happens there?*

S: When the people on that circular ring want to meet from time to time, there are meeting halls at the four directions around the ring. The north, south, east and west villages all have their own meeting halls. We are in the south village, and we gather at our meeting hall to discuss and see if people want to change some aspect of our lives. And we meet to celebrate when people get married or children are born or reach special times in their lives.

J: *And what do you do in your leisure time? Do you have hobbies or pastimes?*

S: I play a musical instrument, like a flute.

J: *So you make your own music and entertainment?*

S: People play music, or dance and sing, or play board games with counters, and these games are circular in shape. And there's storytelling. I would say, singing, playing music, and storytelling are our three main amusements. Most people play some kind of musical instrument, a flute or stringed instrument, and there are special instruments that have crystals in them and produce a sound when you pass your hand over them.

J: *In this lifetime did you ever get seriously ill?*

S: Yes, there was one occasion when I fell and broke my leg. I was somewhat in a fever because it took time to get me to the proper temple, as the temple in our area could not deal with this. So I was taken quite a journey on a transport to another temple. There I was surrounded by a number of people using crystals. They placed crystals all around me and they had crystals in their hands. I was drifting in and out of consciousness, and I don't remember clearly what they did. But I do remember they used clear crystals mainly, but some of the crystals they held were colored. They projected colored light over my leg, too, but I don't know how they did that. It was quite a process, but the bones knitted together very well.

J: *And were you married in this life?*

S: Yes, and we had children, a girl and a boy.

J: *And did your children have a general education, or were they assessed quite early on as having special talents?*

S: There was an attunement to assess the skills they had developed in past lives. They had a general education, but on top of that, they received special training where it was needed. My son, who was talented in music and would probably become a musician, was given special tuition in that direction. My daughter is interested in crystals and may go on to become a Priestess in one of the temples. I'm not sure if she will do healing work or use crystals in other ways, it's too early to say. So they are given extra instruction to develop those skills, but everyone gets a general education as well. We are all taught the basic things, the Great Laws, the focus on Oneness, and so on. Eventually my daughter will go to a temple that specializes in training in crystals, and my son will go to one that develops the musical skills, but that is for the future. They are young yet.

J: *Do you have animals as pets?*

S: Yes, my children both have a pet dog. The pets usually appear when the child is born. They exist in the wooded areas and appear when the child is born to be both their guardian and companion. They don't need to talk to their pets, of course; they have telepathic communication. Telepathy is used very widely although speech is used on occasions, too. If there is a public gathering, speech will be used so that it should all be clear from the beginning. But in small groups, telepathy is more common. It gets complicated if you've got large groups, and everyone is producing ideas at the same time. And then you can become confused about who is producing which thought. That is why when there are public announcements to large numbers of people, it's always done in speech. In small groups when it's obvious who is thinking, telepathy is more widely used.

J: *Can you take me forward to another important event in that lifetime?*

S: One of the children of the village has qualified to become a Priest in a temple some distance from here, so we all go to mark this. The whole village turns out to see him in his new temple. The children are considered to be the children of the whole community and not the children of just one family. So it's an important time for the whole village, and we go to celebrate his success. So this is a big event for all of us, and we feel good about that.

J: *Are there any other significant journeys that you make?*

S: There is one major journey that I make to the big Temple in the Central City. I am quite old by then, and my wife goes with me. We see the Temple, a beautiful temple, very high—you can see it a long way off. It is very beautifully made, and there is an area that only the priests can go into because you have to levitate to get into it. We know there are people with special abilities like levitation, and we honor these people. They have worked up to that; perhaps, in previous lives they worked up to the use of these skills.

At the Temple we see a very powerful leader, one of the founders of our civilization. He seems to be surrounded by an energy field so that his form changes according to who is looking at him. I see him as a wise old man, but I am told that others see him differently.

J: *What happens on occasions like these?*

S: We gather below the temple, and there is a ceremony as we climb up towards the temple, and the wise leader speaks. Well, he both speaks and produces telepathy at the same time, so he's giving us various levels of teaching.

J: *Is this teaching to do with your spiritual life?*

S: Yes. He's teaching us to move through responsibility and intention towards a greater degree of Oneness. All the strands of our consciousness and all the efforts we make on our path lead to Oneness. And in a sense this big Temple is the supreme symbol of Oneness, the hub of the whole Atlantean system. The Priests who work in this Temple are not working for themselves but for the

49

greater Oneness and the experience of that truth—that all life is connected. That we are one another. That there is no real separation—only apparent separation.

So that was an important day for us. But you cannot understand these great Beings like the leaders; they are far beyond us. They have powers and abilities that we couldn't even begin to imagine. Eventually, we will grow and develop such abilities, but we haven't reached that level yet.

J: *And do you have more of a spirituality than a religion?*

S: There are spiritual laws, and the Priests and Priestesses are regarded as spiritual beings, not religious beings. There is no sense of a hierarchy exploiting the people below it. The Priests and Priestesses are simply people of a higher consciousness and higher technical abilities, abilities in the use of energy and consciousness. They are not interceding between us and the Source because we all have a connection with the Source, and, in fact, part of their work is to encourage us to make that connection stronger. So there is no sense of the Priests and Priestesses having a unique ability to contact the Source that no one else has. Our tradition is a spiritual system, a way of treading a spiritual path, a way of living rather than a religion.

J: *How would you sum up the experience of this life on Atlantis?*

S: It was a gentle time, no competition, no rivalry. There was no sense of anyone trying to push himself/herself forward or trying to be above anyone else. All worked together for the good of all with everything pointing towards an essential Oneness that we all shared. It was a most satisfying life, but it wasn't dramatic. There were not many crises although I did break my leg. Mostly it was a peaceful life, full of quiet satisfactions and the warmth of friendship and the feeling that we are all working in harmony for the greater good.

8.

Shared Lives

For most of the past lives that we investigate there is only one subject involved, although we did give examples of two subjects regressed together in *The Essenes, Children of the Light*. This next session was unusual because three subjects were involved, all reliving a shared past life experience at the time of Golden Atlantis.

The opportunity to review a past life shared by three people does not present itself very often, but it does occur. The big advantage of experiencing a shared past life is that we can get different perspectives on the same event, as no two people living through an experience would see it in exactly the same way. And we have found that the group energy works to stimulate the memory so that details are recovered that otherwise might be lost. Taking part in this session, which was held in February 2006, were Catherine Mary La Toure, Joanna and Stuart.

Catherine Mary: There are some people milling around in a wide open space. They are wearing pale pink, pale blue, and white robes, sleeveless, gathered at the waist and going right down to the ground. It's as if a ceremony is being held. We're here to perform a ritual, and there is a large quartz crystal pyramid near to us all. It doesn't seem to have an entrance in it.

Joanna: I'm seeing the open space, and I feel there's a temple in the background. I'm very familiar with this place.

Stuart: Yes, it's as if we're in a big square, and the crystal pyramid is in the middle of the square and on the far side there is this temple, a very beautiful temple with columns.

C: We come for ritual, but it seems that we are onlookers rather than taking part in it.

S: Yes, it feels as if I'm in the audience.

C: Why are we watching?

S: We're here to witness this in some way.

C: It feels good. The people in the square seem to be quite happy to be waiting here. We seem to be waiting for a signal from the crystal. It seems to be linked to the sun shining on the top of the crystal. When that happens, the crystal gives off a very sharp laser-like beam. Now the people seem to be gathering into more organized groups.

S: I think when the light strikes the very top of the crystal, the point of it, the capstone, which seems to be made of a different material, then starts to glow. And it makes a sound, too. And I think the note it produces is taken up by the people around it—we begin to sing the same note.

C: The people we are looking at (pause) they seem to have in each of the groups a smaller crystal. These small crystals are held in the hand and seem to be resonating with the pyramid, bringing the sound and the light into their own space. They seem to be looking at the pyramid very intently.

J: The sound is a vibration: it activates the smaller crystals.

C: Why?

S: It's as if the big crystal is talking in a way to the other crystals. It's communicating with them.

C: Why are we watching and not taking part?

S: I think they're practicing something, some form of tuning in or attunement.

C: A reddish purple light seems to be spreading round the group. It seems to be giving them some sort of help. It doesn't come from the point of the crystal; it comes from lower down and it comes round to the right and round the back of the people and encircles them in a kind of whirlwind of color. It seems to be an energy from the stars. That's what we've been waiting for, planets and stars to be aligned.

S: It's a different, very strong healing energy. This is helping the bodies to be in the peak of health. But it's also a remembrance of some deep connection with a star system.

C: It's almost as if the red and purple color was coming round the people like a spiral galaxy.

S: Yes, almost like a little vortex. It's swirling around all the people, and, I wouldn't say healing them, more maintaining the health they have.

J: I also feel it's getting everyone in alignment.

S: Yes.

J: So that we can all act as one, the individual merged into Oneness.

C: What is this group doing that has a bearing on the future? It seems to be uniting and realigning. Is that in our bodies or our chakras?

J: I would say heart, mind and soul.

C: Looking at the people (pause) they seem to be directly connecting with their higher selves. While the triangle of the pyramid is pointing upwards, they seem to have a triangle of energy pointing downwards around the top part of their bodies down to their hearts.

S: Like a big funnel really.

C: Yes, almost as if they are feeding on the energy and pulling in a particular signal.

S: Yes.

C: The whole energy seems to be red and purple (pause) it's difficult to see what's going on as the energy swirling around is so intense.

S: I think this pyramid is aligned with a particular star system, and there are other pyramids elsewhere that are aligned with other star systems.

C: Which star system is this aligned with?

S: I think this is Sirius.

J: Yes, that's what I got.

C: And just as you said that—I didn't think there were any doors in the pyramid, but the side of it just opened up and a creature like Anubis walked out, not on four legs but on two.

There was a pause and a shift in the energy of the group.

C: Now I'm seeing a place that is high up a mountain, and the top of the mountain has been flattened. The people here have different energies from the people down below.

J: I feel we have been brought forward in time as you say that. We started further down, and now there's a group of us that have gone further up.

S: Yes. It was a square before but now...

J: We've changed our location.

S: There is another pyramid here, but it's smaller.

J: But we're still connected with the people down in the square. Somehow the energy flows between the two sites.

S: It's all part of a grid, and this is the Sirius grid, and I think there are other star systems and other grids as well.

J: Yes.

C: The air is full of beings of a subtler level than the third dimension (pause) there are all sorts of different people, people with lion faces and narrow eyes, people with huge dragonfly wings, like gossamer but much larger than a dragonfly.

St: It seems as if every form you could imagine is present here.

C: It's as if they've come to watch something very special.

Once again there was a sense of the energy shifting.

J: Now we've moved forward and here there is some kind of initiation going to happen (pause) something to do with the Order of Melchizedek.

S: We've shifted to a temple, a really big temple.

C: We've come inside, and there are lots of pillars with writing on them.

S: And some of the images of those creatures with strange faces are on these pillars, but their energy is also floating around here too. They are present in many forms.

C: The air is now pink and a vibrant orange. This temple almost feels Egyptian but not quite.

S: It does feel like an Egyptian temple, yes.

C: There's certainly a Horus-like bird which is way on top of one of the pillars, looking down.

S: We're looking up through the main hall of the temple which stretches before us, and up a few steps there is a Priestess and she is holding up a pyramid—crystalline and a pale translucent green, about as high as a hand is long.

C: Green is a symbol for connections through the heart.

S: There's a lot of sound here, a lot of singing. There are a number of people dispersed around the pillars, and they're singing.

C: I get the name Anawar for the Priestess. There seems to be a lot of imagery around wings.

S: Yes, wings and the possibility of levitating.

Once again there was an energy shift within the group.

C: I'm not getting the image of the Priestess any longer. We seem to have moved on. I think we've reached a stage where we no longer venerate images of people because I can see a ledge, a kind of altar, but there's no effigy or icon on it.

S: Is this sometime later?

C: Yes, the green crystal pyramid has become a lot bigger now.

S: And it has got its own resting place. Now it's on a plinth, the base of a column. This is a smaller temple, and the inside is made of white marble with gold columns around it.

C: The people here are wearing white and gold, white robes with gold bands around the waist and gold clasps around our upper arms.

S: So it's a white marble temple with gold columns and people clad in white mainly but with gold ornaments.

J: I'm getting confused with this because the women are wearing exactly the same as the men.

C: There doesn't seem to be any great difference in size or shape between men and women. They do seem to be very androgynous.

S: I think this is an androgynous 'priesthood' or 'priestesshood'—there isn't a word for it.

J: Is everything balanced like this?

S: No, this is just one Order. This is not what the great bulk of the population is like.

C: But this is really quite late in Atlantean history.

S: Yes, this is much later, probably a high peak in the Golden Age when the energies have perfected, and everything is brought to a much greater balance. This isn't what all the people can manage. This is a very special Order which has brought balance to a very high level—balance in everything from the physical level

56

right up to consciousness. And it's really taking the energies we saw earlier and developing that heart energy to its peak. I think the great mass of the people are male and female, but in this temple there is a complete balance. In this Order they've worked up to this balance and evolved towards it. This was an aspirational gender, not identical with the main evolution but something that came from it. If one evolved over a number of Atlantean lives and focused on balance, this was the result of all that arc of achievement.

We realized that through Alariel we might be able to access deeper understanding of the events we had witnessed, so immediately after the group session, we went into dialogue with him. Alariel was able to give us a commentary on the process that we had experienced, revealing layers of meaning that enabled us to put all this into a much bigger perspective.

C: *What were those people really doing when we went to the first scene in Atlantis with the crystal pyramid? We thought it was to maintain health.*

Alariel: Partly. But they were holding their own individual little pyramids, and these pyramids were gathering information, encodements, and vibrations from the central pyramid which was aligned with Sirius. They would then take their little pyramids and go back to their villages and teach about Sirius through letting people tune in to these little pyramids. They would say, "You can experience Sirus. This is what Sirius is like. Just tune in to this little pyramid."

C: *Why would they need to do that?*

A: Because it was not always possible for the children who grew up in villages to understand what another star system was like. You could talk about a star system, but it was not always easy to be aware of what that system felt like. What did it feel like to be a Sirian? That's what they wanted to convey. How did the Sirian civilization feel to the Sirians and what quality did it have? Using these pyramids was their way of having a direct experience of a star system, and others would come at different times with pyramids attuned to other star systems. So the pyramids were a teaching vehicle, but not in an academic sense—the information was qualitative rather than quantitative.

All the children of Golden Atlantis had the opportunity to tune in to these small pyramid-shaped crystals and experience what it was like to be on Sirius, or Arcturus, Andromeda, Orion and so on. But for those who belonged to this particular soul family, there were separate sessions when only children from their own soul family were present, so that these brothers and sisters from, say, Sirius, could attune more powerfully with their "home" energy. There would often be tears of joy in the eyes of these children at these special gatherings, and afterwards they would all hug one another as long-lost but newly-found brothers and sisters of the Sirius soul family.

Because the people of Golden Atlantis were so closely attuned to their own origin, the original star system from which they came, they made a conscious effort to reconnect with the energy of that star system. This nourished them at a profound spiritual level. They spent regular time connecting with their soul family across the cosmos, their brothers and sisters in what your Native Americans would call "Sky Nation." Through that regular reconnection, they knew at a very deep level who they were. The link between two individuals in the same star soul family can be very profound, and some of the deepest levels of friendship amongst the new children can be explained within this context.

J: *Who was the Priestess we saw in one of the Atlantean temples, the one we identified as Anawar?*

A: That Priestess was one of the incarnations of Jeshua. There has been much written about the male past lives of Jeshua, including Adam and the father of Zoroaster. These are both remarkable lives, but they tell only a part of Jeshua's story. By associating him—in his past-life forms—exclusively with a male image, the true power and wisdom of the feminine energy has been denied.

J: *What work did we do with Jeshua in Atlantis that has relevance to our lives today?*

A: Jeshua in his Atlantean Priestess form was bringing down the Cosmic energy of Love, but this energy was fully experienced in Golden Atlantis by only a few people because only a few at that time had the essential balance to take it on board and fully attune to it. This Priestess was attempting to bring in the energy of unconditional Love from way across the galaxy right outside your solar system. She was attempting to focus and stabilize it—not anchor it yet, that wasn't possible because too few people were ready for it—but just to stabilize it so that those Initiates who were ready at that time, who had moved on in their consciousness and were prepared to make the sacrifices necessary to achieve complete balance, could resonate with it and begin to work with it in their lives. So this Priestess was opening a doorway, a portal so that this energy could come through to Earth for the first time and could be accessed and worked with in a practical way for the first time by these few advanced ones.

A number of these same advanced Initiates gathered again two thousand years ago when the time finally came for anchoring this energy. They worked as

Essenes and supported Jeshua, their Teacher, the same Teacher who as this Priestess had begun this energy process all those centuries before in Atlantis.

So the energy was brought in first and stabilized in Atlantis, but it wasn't possible to anchor it in the energy field of the Earth at that time so that many people could access it.

C: *Please tell us more about this energy and the balance involved with it.*

A: This is the energy of completely balanced unconditional Love with the balance being so complete that there would never be a wobbling over into any kind of conditionality. So whether someone smiled at you or snarled at you, it would make absolutely no difference to you because the balance was perfect within you, and you would act from that point of balance, a balance that could not be disturbed by anyone or any situation.

That was so difficult for people to achieve during the Atlantean period. Even during the Golden Age, they saw things in personal and family terms, and that meant they were not completely unconditional because they wished their family well to a greater degree than others they were not related to. So at that time most people on Atlantis could not manage total unconditionality. There were many wonderful achievements during Golden Atlantis, but totally unconditional Love was not something reached by the great mass of the population—achieved by a few Priests and Priestesses, yes, but not by the whole of the population.

This was such a new energy, so strange, so transpersonal, that it had to come into human consciousness and human experience gradually. So it was necessary first to stabilize it, and this was done in the Priestess life of Jeshua. When he returned two thousand years ago, human development had moved on. It was not that the general vibrational level of humanity had risen. Indeed you could say that at this point in the Roman era, it had slipped back. What was different was the number of individuals who were starting to wake up spiritually and were ready to function as independent, spiritually-responsible adults. Though there were quite a number of advanced spiritual adults on Atlantis, the great mass of the population were still children spiritually. They were gentle, loving, accepting, intelligent, creative, yes, but not strong enough yet to stand on their own spiritual feet, think and decide for themselves, and resolutely carve out their own pathway to the Light.

But in Israel two thousand years ago a number of people were ready to take that leap forward. It was appropriate then for Jeshua to anchor the energy of unconditional Love so that everyone who was open to change could work with it and begin to understand it. But the complete balance of unconditionality was difficult for even these advanced ones who worked alongside Jeshua, mainly in the Essene movement at that time, and it continues to be challenging to human beings, doesn't it?

It is not an easy thing to be totally unconditional because then you look at every life-form with the eyes of Father-Mother God, a completely balanced perception, loving all and condemning none. This completely balanced perception is at once involved and detached, personal and transpersonal—ah, how long it has taken humanity to work up towards that!

The white temple you saw in Golden Atlantis was the peak of much effort to achieve this kind of balance in support of bringing this energy in, but it was a minority effort as most people weren't ready for it. This was so new a balance to humanity at that time that it expressed itself in ways that were not necessary as time went on, and the essence of that balance was better understood and could be more practically applied. At that time it was perceived that a concentration on an androgyne energy focus was necessary to achieve that balance because the complication of gender would be taken out of the equation entirely. Later it became possible to focus that energy regardless of one's orientation, but that was a later and more sophisticated stage in dealing with this energy.

This Androgyne Order on Atlantis also worked to balance the left and right halves of the brain in order to bridge and connect these halves so that the brain could work as a complete and interconnected whole. This Order was only a stage in bringing in this energy, and no other civilization after Atlantis needed to pursue this particular path to unconditional balance. What is needed now in achieving this balance is to focus on transpersonal consciousness. Because that's how Father-Mother God sees all beings: lovingly with complete acceptance and transpersonally with no favoring one being over another.

In a way the Androgyne Order was an echoing of something much older, the civilization on Lemuria which was certainly androgynous at any rate in its earliest stages. But then Lemuria was not so densely physical as Atlantis - at that point people floated over the ground rather than walking solidly upon it.

C: *Is Hawaii part of this Lemurian culture?*

A: Yes, it's the outer fringe of Lemuria. You sense the feminine energy when you go to Hawaii, it's softer, gentler, isn't it?

C: *Yes. The Goddess of the Volcano, Pele is depicted as a woman.*

A: Yes. Pele is not always gentle I have to say—Ah, she is laughing! She is gentle when that is appropriate, but when it is necessary for a volcano to erupt under her guidance, there is not always gentleness in the eruption process!

C: *What should this group learn to use from this trip to Atlantis today ?*

A: To be conscious of the overall arc of history. These events were a long time ago, but they fit in perfectly to the pattern which led, first of all, to the Essene work and, secondly, to today. You're still working on the basic energy of unconditional Love at this time. Some have completely mastered it, but relatively few, we would say. Most people are still working on that. They may have learned to be balanced in their minds, but to be totally balanced in the heart center and in the emotional body, that's harder for most people.

J: *And why is Golden Atlantis relevant today?*

A: Golden Atlantis is relevant now because you're currently in the process of becoming the beings that you were then. But there's a difference. Then you did it naturally but unconsciously, like a loving and obedient child. Now you are learning to touch and sustain the same high vibrational level as a fully conscious and responsible adult. Then you were the children being taught. Now you are becoming the teachers and going on to teach and lead others. Golden Atlantis tapped into your potential as empowered Beings of Light but in a natural, instinctive childlike way. Now you can realize that potential consciously, and that high vibrational achievement will be yours forever.

In Golden Atlantis you visited the paradise of high vibrational life. Now in the New Age and the New World, you will enjoy it as a permanent experience. Atlantis was the fleeting potential. Now you are fast approaching the full and permanent realization.

9.

A Temple Complex

We had heard that the temple complexes in Golden Atlantis were particularly beautiful and wanted more information on them. Although there were temples in some of the Atlantean villages, the big temple complexes were said to be found within a city environment.

The first life we accessed with Stuart on Golden Atlantis was a mostly rural experience, but fortunately we found another life during this period which was city-based. At that time Stuart was an artist called Orintha, and when we asked him to choose a particularly interesting sequence of temples and describe them for us, this is how the session progressed:

Orintha: There was one temple complex that impressed me above all others. It was not the largest or the grandest, but it had the biggest diversity and creative variety. As you entered the main hall, you found that it was circular in shape and airy and cool with light coming down from the roof that was changing color as great crystals set high above reflected different aspects of the spectrum of sunlight. Along one side of the main hall, there was a corridor leading to seven rooms, which were bathed in seven colors.

The first of the color rooms is red with a couch in the center bathed in rose red light from a crystal in the ceiling. You could lie upon this couch and be bathed in pink light, and crystals are amplifying the color streaming down. The person I could see on the couch looked pale and anemic. Most people might have a fairly quick top-up of energy by coming to this room, and only the more severe cases would need to spend a long time here. This person had lost a lot of blood and needed much time here to recover.

People are sensitive enough to the color to know how much they need of this rose red light, and are able to monitor their own healing. A healer was in attendance and was ensuring that the patient did not receive too much of this strong color energy. The music in the background was like organ music, a strong and noble chorale.

We went into the next room, which was orange, and in this case, the patient was sitting rather than lying down. The orange light coming down from the ceiling crystal was very strong, and I was told by the healer there it was particularly suitable for cases involving the spleen. There was gentle string music in the background, rising and falling softly like waves.

The next room we moved into was a pale yellow. Here the patient was lying on a couch and seemed to have some form of liver trouble. The light coming from the ceiling crystal was yellow, and the walls and floor are also yellow, so that everything in the room resonated with that color. The healer here wore yellow robes, but the patient on the couch wore a white, light flowing robe with a cord round the waist.

The music here was longer chords, more sustained. It is like a choir of many voices sustaining long chords, and sometimes a part within the chord changed and that shifted the quality of the music. There was no visible source of this music in any of these rooms.

We moved on to the green room, a green with a little blue in it. Here the patient had a heart condition. The music here was slow, soothing, instrumental and very pastoral in feeling. On one side of the room there is a big crystal with a number of smaller crystals around it, and as the music swelled I could see the light increase within the crystals. And the crystals themselves sang and added overtones to the music.

We moved on to the blue room, a beautiful strong blue, deep and rich. The music was cool, like flutes, quite light and airy in its effect. The patient here was sitting down and has some florid or feverish condition.

On then into the indigo room, where the light was a very dark blue. The patient was lying on a couch, and the music was like a high-pitched string instrument, very strong but also sweet and soothing, too.

The last room was violet, quite a fine strong violet color. The patient here was lying down, and the music was majestic and soulful, both instruments and a voice, quite slow and moving. The effect was calming and reassuring, as if drawing all into the greater Oneness.

That completes the description of one cluster of seven rooms grouped around the central hall.

And that hall led to a further sequence of seven rooms.

The first room was all white, and the patient was lying down on a couch with a pyramid suspended above. Crystals were placed in pairs on either side of the body to correspond with chakra points, and there was one large crystal sphere at the head and one at the feet. The crystals were clear, but had many colors pulsing through them, so you could call this the rainbow room, a place of cleansing and toning up.

When we went into the next room, it is in darkness, a rich indigo darkness with silver stars all around. When you would lie on the central couch this space opened up a direct channel to a specific star you wish to focus on. This was an attunement and communication room for astronomers and seers. It reconnected the person to his/her star system of origin and is a source of great strength and star-wisdom.

The next room was very different, full of bright light. This was the sun room, with rays reaching out all around from the middle of the ceiling. There were suns painted all around the walls, and the color changed from the pale dawning sun to the rich golden orange of the setting sun. You would lie on the central couch and tune in to any aspect of the sun you wanted. This room had a warm, expansive feeling to it.

The next room was silvery, for this was the moon room. The images shimmered into one another right round the beautiful blue walls with silvery moons and various aspects of the moon. Surrounding the central couch was a moat of water, crossed by a little set of steps. The whole room had a dreamlike quality, and people came here to help in understanding their dreams. They tuned in to the essence of the moon and that revealed the meaning of the dream for them, a meaning which could be as much based in feelings as in thoughts.

The next room had a number of trees growing round the walls, and the couch in the middle had roots coming out of it and growing along the floor to connect with the walls. This was the earth room, and there were roots and branches everywhere. Lying on the couch the individual tuned in to the energies of the earth. People who needed grounding came here.

In the next room there was water everywhere, and water symbols covered the walls. In this water room the water flowed and cascaded down into dishes and pools. There was a couch in the middle, and some lighting effect gave the illusion that you were wading through waves to get to the couch. Lying on the couch was like being rocked by the waves deep below the sea. Everything flowed and you felt deeply supported and nourished. It was like a lullaby at the bottom of the ocean while being rocked in the cradle of the sea. As you looked up to the ceiling, you could see the sun shining on the top of the waves above you.

The last room was air with paintings of air-spirits on the walls, and the floor was shaped like the top of a mountain so it was possible to climb up to the central couch and lie down there. It was a good place to let the winds blow and make everything fresh and clear and a good place for tuning in and getting clarity on the next steps in one's life. As the powerful wind blew there, it swept away all internal rubbish, and left a person stronger and clearer, pared down like a stone blown clean by the winds.

And that completed the second sequence of seven rooms in this most interesting temple complex.

J: *How are people chosen to work in these temples?*

O: In these temple complexes, it is not so much a hierarchy as a question of vibration. You do work according to your vibrational level, so the people with higher vibrations are those doing the more complex and subtle healing work. This is the pattern throughout Atlantis—you are assessed for your work according to your vibrational level.

10.

The Diversity of Healing

Another shared pastlife session with Catherine Mary gave us a different perspective on the Atlantean healing temples. This chapter makes an interesting comparison with the previous one and underlines the great variety of ways in which the Atlanteans used color and sound.

Catherine Mary: The temples in this area are quite Greek in terms of architecture. As you go in, there are several tall pillars and they're made of clear crystal that looks like glass. They're wide at the bottom and narrower at the top, almost like an elongated bud of a waterlily or lotus. They're cool and very calming. If you put the flat of your hand or the side of your face on them, it feels very soothing ... as if you've come home to a place with no worries.

Joanna: I sense this building is on a bed of crystal, and the crystal is creating an energetic exchange with these pillars. I think the column is connected to a crystalline structure underneath.

C: You don't even feel that you want to let go of the pillars until you're ready, so you hold on to them until the crystal is ready to release you (pause) now there's an energy pulse that appears to be shooting up through the middle of the pillar, and as you hold it you get a feeling of energy moving upwards. And it feels as if you won't be able to hold onto the pillar much longer because you've activated it, and it's no longer cool and calming.

J: I think as we come in, there's an area where we change from our outside garb. We're a bit dusty as we come in and we don't want to bring the dust into this place, so we slip out of our clothes and get into these fresh white robes because there's such a feeling of keeping this place clean and pure.

C: They smell nice. They smell of roses. They're not actually my clothes, but they fit.

J: It's a type of loose robe.

C: We go through into this darker chamber, and there seems to be something in the ceiling that we're being made aware of. It seems to be a crystal which is triangular in shape at the top and comes down to a point at the bottom, and there seems to be within it a white being who has her hands out. Maybe she is the energy of the crystal or the angel of the crystal.

Now I can see three beds which are obviously for us. They seem to be overlaid with petals and symbols, and we make ourselves comfortable on these beds. Now we're surrounded by a lot of white, it's a rejuvenation process as well as a healing process.

Stuart: So there's a concentration of white light.

C: Yes, and the back of the beds are slightly raised. The energy seems to be healing the source of our beginning rather than us. So it's almost like an x-ray machine but instead of looking at the bone health, it's looking at the DNA health. These healing beds could be used for anyone with a DNA defect, but with us it's looking to see how our human template is working with our non-human origins. Many people from different realms came in to see what Earth was like to live on as a physical dimension, and so these ethereal planets are adjusting the balance between their DNA and human

DNA in case anything goes out of balance because the templates are quite unlike one another.

We're ready to get off the beds now. That was quite a dark room. Nothing else was in it, except this one crystal. Now we're being taken back to the outer chamber.

J: My sense is that we've gone into a brighter area. A series of circular rooms. My sense is my work is much more to do with energies and sound.

S: There are special temples connected with sound, and some of them are quite elaborate structures so that sound could be experienced in the best possible way. In some of these, the patient lies in a large shell-like structure, and the waves of sound wash over him. He experiences all kinds and frequencies of sound. Some are very low sounds where the vibration seems to come up from the ground, and high-pitched sounds, and many sounds between the two.

J: I feel very related to the sound chambers, but I feel there were many ways of working with sound. One way is when there is a person in the middle, and there's a circle of people around. They have crystals, and by projecting energy, the crystals start to sing, and the people use their voices to harmonize with the crystals and make this a wonderful sound bath, and it harmonizes the person sitting in the middle of this sound bath.

There was a pause and a shift in the energy of the group.

C: Now I'm seeing a completely different place. Quite private, and you just have to know about it. A sacred site but further up the mountain. You ascend to it in a craft, an interesting-looking craft, it's shaped like a sting-ray, and it's swimming through the air. These craft seem to be opaque but also slightly see-through. You can see the occupants in them. And there seem to be lines of energy that you can go on, so you can't collide with other craft. There's a pattern of energy going one way, and a pattern of energy going another way. And it takes you up to a quite spectacular crystal castle, but I'm going when the sun isn't yet on it. We're going early in the morning, just before the dawn, so it's quite quiet. The sky is grey and pink, and this seems to be the best time—it's to do with the currents in the air. So this is a weekly trip to rebalance the energies.

J: It gives you a feel-good factor.

C: Yes, it's just getting back to yourself and getting yourself rebalanced, so you could have some sunshine energy if you wanted or have the chakras rebalanced. But there's no such thing here as massage. No one touches anyone. They don't need to.

J: Yes, because we are much more in our Light Bodies, and we aren't so physical.

C: I'm quite keen on the color chamber. I like the colors. But here I'm not seeing crystals, I'm seeing amazing flowers, and light is shining through the flowers, and the light increases their energy and they give off perfume—it's wonderful. So purple perfume... it's quite "violety." Red is quite a heavy perfume. I don't recognize it. Turquoise is a beautiful lily of the valley type of perfume. Carnations for pink, and white is like a ginger. You're also going to get the healing lights, but you begin with perfume. The perfume goes straight into the brain and puts you into the mood for healing. It goes straight into the energy centers in the brain and has the purpose of linking the physical with the etheric and the etheric with the other realms, so you're ready to receive higher healing. So that's why you always get the perfume first.

Now we're going on to the color. I need something done with my eyes, so I'm getting a violet light. It helps people who are ageing and who are having trouble with their vision. Now I'm seeing a very rich purple light which doesn't shine in my eyes at all; it just IS in my eyes. It's there. I'm seeing purple light, but nothing is actually shining on me.

S: So the light is generated in quite a gentle way.

C: Hmm... I feel you also get the sound of that chakra coming through. As you get the violet light the sound goes straight into the crown chakra . And now the color is turning to pink. This pink is quite a stimulating color, stimulating the heart. It seems to be encouraging the heart to beat regularly. It's quite a bright magenta pink ... people would need this as they got older just to keep the heart going on the physical level. They have this work with color and light down to a fine art, very advanced.

There was another pause here, and a shift in energy.

J: Now we're entering a big circular building with a domed roof divided into segments, each of which is a different color like a stained-glass window, and the sun shines through on to the people below. And you can either have just one color, or a combination of colors because there are blinds that can block off the colors. So it's a single-color system, but it is multi-faceted, too.

Comment by Stuart: What we get here in this session is the impression of a number of different techniques, each of them finely tuned to the needs of the patient on a specific level. It is clear that the physical body was perceived by the Atlanteans during the Golden Era as one level within a holistic system of being, and there was a methodical approach to dealing with each of the subtle levels in an appropriate and effective way. This remarkably progressive and holistic approach to human well-being adds up to a very advanced system that encompassed both healing and health-maintenance. Clearly such a complex system would not have been a quick or easy thing to put in place, and it must have developed through a long period of research and practical application.

11.

The Arts of Atlantis

Alariel: It is difficult to communicate the essential quality of the arts on Atlantis during the Golden Age, yet since the arts were such a vital part of Atlantean society, we shall try to convey at least some impression of them.

Most of the major arts you currently recognize flourished during Golden Atlantis, but they operated within a framework of self-discipline and self-restraint that a modern society might find very strange indeed. Let us take poetry as a example. One of the leading poets of Golden Atlantis was called Kayden; he developed a general statement of what poetry should be, a statement that attracted very wide approval throughout the artistic world at that time. Here is an extract from the central part of that statement:

Poetry should reflect
the creativity of the personality,
the light of the soul
and the fire of the Spirit.

The four pillars of poetry
are Beauty and Truth,
Love and Light.
When poetry reflects these ideals,
it adds to the happiness of the world

and helps the heart to sing.
Beauty in poetry
is not only a beauty of word and form
but a beauty of thought and feeling.
Poetry should not contain
any trace of violence or cruelty,
harshness or anger, damage or despair.

These things are ugly,
and it is the duty of every poet
to avoid the ugly
as if it were a monster,
eating away at the soul of our society.

Ugliness is to be shunned
for its vibration
which is dull and heavy.
Our finest poetry
avoids all heaviness
and soars up
into the lightness of the soul.

Here you can sense the underlying quality of all Atlantean art.
In the Atlantean view, art should point towards a fine ideal, and
possess a spiritual quality. And Kayden continues:

When the poem is powerful and true,
the physical presence of the poet
aligns with his soul
and his Spirit.
Then, while the rhythm of the poem carries him,
he is one whole Being,
an integrated and inspired
Child of the Light.
As Wholeness reflects the essence of the One,
we consider any process like poetry,

or music or dance that unites us with our Wholeness,
to be a sacred thing.

This high idealism was carried forward through all the arts of Atlantis. Dancing, often in groups or circles, would have all the joy and lightness of sacred dance, while the paintings shone with shimmering touches of light and high frequency pale and translucent colors that are only now starting to return to human awareness.

The music of Golden Atlantis was also light and gentle in its character. It used many of the instruments you know today, the pure tones of flutes being greatly valued, but at that time there were also instruments unknown to you. Some of these were made of crystals, and when these sang, they had clear and pure tones that go beyond any instrument known today. And the Atlanteans also had devices that made music when a hand was waved near them and some subtle instruments that would even resonate to the movements in the musician's aura.

The sculpture of Atlantis focused on flowing forms, often with great lightness and delicacy, so that many of these sculptures had the feeling of a bird in flight or a dolphin leaping with joy. Dolphins were a popular motif in Atlantean art and were widely regarded as symbols of joy. When the Atlanteans were asked what they considered to be the most beautiful words, the list that emerged from this process was interesting:

dolphin
rainbow
shimmering
star
crystal
wonder
angel

Here in just seven words you have a little microcosm of Atlantean life, and an insight into the arts of Atlantis.

However, there was one area where the Atlantean arts differed sharply from your present cultural experience: their perception of "drama" was very different from any definition of that word today. In the modern world, drama is based upon conflict and the resolution of that conflict. The conflict can be either internal (within one individual) or external (between individuals or groups). Since the people of Golden Atlantis chose not to focus on conflict or give it any energy, drama in the modern sense did not exist at that time.

Atlantis produced no great novels, but there were plays, and a blend of music and story, but in these the drama rested not upon conflict but on the idea of a journey, a quest that reaches a destination or fulfillment. By modern standards they were very gentle dramas, lacking all conflict, trauma, or extreme emotion, but they did meet the needs of Atlantean society.

As the Atlanteans focused so much on Oneness, this was also reflected in the way their arts blended and overlapped. A typical merging in Atlantis was the blend of singing, instrumental sound, dance and the creation of patterns of movement and geometry that flowed into a greater whole. These patterns were being created at the individual and group levels but also at higher levels that could only be seen from other perspectives, for example, from far above the dancers. They even had a formula to express this:

Vocal sound + instrumental sound + words + movement = a healing process.

The Atlanteans did not have a firm division between the spiritual and the artistic, and many of their greatest writers were also active in producing invocations and affirmations. Here, for example, is a popular Dedication that was used by many young Priests and Priestesses during the ceremony which marked the completion of their training in a Temple:

> I dedicate
> all that is within me
> to the service of the Light.

As they meditated upon the meaning of this Dedication, it became a powerful mantra to lift their vibration and keep them centered in the Light. Within every human being there are three levels: personality, soul, and higher self. The higher self, also called the I AM Presence, is pure Spirit, which is Love and Light. So in saying these words you are really saying:

> I am Light,
> and I dedicate the Light that I am
> in service to the Light
> within all beings.

Light was a powerful symbol for the Atlanteans. They used it widely in their art, and it formed a central focus to inspire them in their spiritual life.

12.

The Atlanteans and Landscape

Alariel: The Atlanteans had a unique sensitivity to landscape and the effect that landscape has upon human beings. As they believed so strongly in Oneness, they felt themselves to be within the landscape, but also they were aware that the landscape was *within them.* Resonating completely with Oneness, they saw the world within and the world around them as balanced reflections of each other.

This meant that their approach to the animals and birds they encountered was a little different from those shamanic traditions who treat animals as part of a great wisdom tradition with specific lessons to teach us. With the Native Americans, for example, it is the species of animal—bear or wolf, for instance—that is important, as each teaches different lessons. The Atlanteans did not focus on the species at all but on the *essence* of an animal. Thus, the delicate footsteps of a little bear cub might teach grace while the sad howling of a wolf might speak of loneliness in being without a partner to share the path of life.

So with the Atlanteans, it was how the animals *behaved* when you encountered them and how their actions and their visual impact brought out an understanding in your consciousness, a feeling in your heart, a wisdom in your soul.

Comment by Stuart: Alariel is describing quite a different approach here from the oracle systems that are now so widely used. In the *Medicine Cards* by Jamie Sams and David Carson, for example, bear gives the power of introspection whilst wolf is the pathfinder and teacher of new ideas.

The session with Alariel continues.

A: Because the Atlanteans felt such a complete integration with the landscape, that also meant that the elements within the landscape spoke directly to them in a way that a modern city-dweller would find difficult to understand.

     For the Atlantean, every river was an opportunity to explore the nature of flow, every sunrise was a new beginning, and every mountain was a hymn to the power of endurance. A tree bending in the wind might speak to the Atlantean of flexibility, rain might suggest the freshness of purification and renewal, and the rainbow would bring a promise of all the radiant wonder of the Light.

     The Atlantean experienced Oneness in the landscape through feeling both the power and quality of life-energy as it flowed from the All to the individual and back again to the All. Thus, the whole cycle of flow and Oneness was recognized. and acknowledged in Atlantean culture in a way that goes far beyond modern understanding.

     One catches a glimpse of this in the mantra, *Om mani padme hum,* but this is so little understood now that the profound Oneness implied in it is almost forgotten. When Atlantis had completed its whole cycle and the time of its final destruction came, the wise teachers of Atlantis took their followers by ship and then overland to new locations all around the world. A few reached even that remote area which you know as Tibet and seeded the wisdom tradition there. That is why this mantra has such deep roots. And this is what the mantra really means:

Om is the One.
Mani is the mind, or more precisely "consciousness."
Padme is the creative flowering (literally, "the lotus.")
Hum is the essence (literally, the "perfume.")

And when you put all these elements together, the true meaning of this mantra emerges:

From the One arises consciousness.
From consciousness arises the creative flowering.
From the creative flowering arises the essence,
     which returns again to the One.

This is a description of the process of life, and it is consistent at every level throughout the whole of Creation. Thus, it is a formula which can apply to everything, from a man to a universe. When the creative flowering of a single human life is completed, the essence of that life returns to the soul. When the creative flowering of a solar system is completed, the essence of that life returns to the galaxy. When the creative flowering of a universe is completed, the essence of that life returns to Great Mystery, which is the All. So every form of life arises like a flower, blossoms for a time, and then returns to the One. That is why Oneness is the nature of all that is and *that* is what the Atlanteans understood so deeply and experienced when they walked out in the landscape.

13.

The Significance of Golden Atlantis

Alariel: Golden Atlantis, the most advanced civilization that the Earth has ever seen, was guided by wise and loving Beings of high spiritual attainment. Atlantis during this Golden Age demonstrated the very peak of human existence. No other era came near it for the perfection of its civilization and the deep connection of the individual with the One, the All, which was universally respected and honored. The harmony of the individual reflected the harmony of the whole society, and this echoed the harmony of the One in a way that gave life a special quality, a feeling of "rightness" which pervaded the lives of everyone who lived there.

One of the leading poets of Golden Atlantis described it like this:

> Atlantis is a perfect dream
> in the mind of God.

And indeed there was a dreamlike quality about it, a sense of everything moving in perfect timing like the unfolding of a great slow movement with the theme sweeping on with an effortless sense of rightness to embrace all and nourish all in a living dream of love and peace and joy. And this was a dream shared by thousands, a perfect dream that miraculously lasted for over a thousand years.

No wonder it made such a deep impression on the collective human consciousness and was etched so deeply on the shared memory that all human beings carry within them. And no wonder it continued to haunt human memory long after all trace of the Atlantean civilization had vanished from the world. For if ever there was a paradise on Earth, this was it.

And such is the power of this collective memory that on one level it will never die. Atlantis will live as long as humanity lives, and Golden Atlantis will continue to evoke deep resonances into the distant future of your race. But now those resonances are particularly powerful, for you have reached an upper point in the spiral of human development that enables you to catch echoes of this earlier period at the same point in the spiral below. That is why Atlantis has become a powerful symbol for you again, and that is why today there is so much interest in all things Atlantean.

When people look back to this high peak of spirituality, they do so for two main reasons: to get information on how this was achieved and inspiration to carry them forward into similar achievements today. We say "similar" because there are major differences between that era and the present day. During Golden Atlantis a small number of leaders were very far ahead of the rest of the population. There was a vast gap between the level of the most advanced consciousness and that of the average person of goodwill.

However, now it is a different picture: large numbers of human beings are waking up and rising to high vibrational levels. Yes, you still have the exceptional advanced souls who inspire and guide you, but now large numbers of people all over the world are stepping into their power and the realization of their true nature as Beings of Light.

The conditions on the planet are also very different now. Gaia has risen substantially in vibration, and that makes your task much easier. All over the world people are responding to the need to reshape their lives so that they live in lighter and more positive ways.

There is a widespread recognition
that the old ways of living have failed
and that a new way has to be found—
a way that honors the Earth,
respects the individual,
and recognizes the importance of the Spirit.

For a long while now, the power of illusion has been strong upon your world, but as your planet rises in vibration and approaches transition, these illusions are now becoming much harder to sustain. For example, when groups of people are greedy, that greed is now quickly exposed for all to see, and the social cost of selfishness is becoming much more widely recognized. This is all part of the process of moving out of the old ways and into a New World with much higher ideals and the possibility of rapid spiritual development for all who are willing to embrace change.

The flame of aspiration burns brightly in many people now, and so it is quite natural for them to think about Golden Atlantis, a period when so many minds and hearts focused on the Light. They draw strength and inspiration from the Atlantean era and go forward with fresh optimism to develop the New Consciousness and play their part in the New World.

Comment by Stuart: I found the passage where Alariel talks about the effortlessness and spontaneity of Atlantean life particularly moving. I recall that the great Japanese potter Shoji Hamada once said that creating a pot should be like "Wandering downhill into a spring breeze." Many people have experienced these "Atlantis moments" when everything flows, and the perfect timing of the stream of life carries us effortlessly along. If this is what life in Golden Atlantis was like, is it any wonder that we want to bring this magical experience back into our lives?

Part Four:

The Atlantean Experiment

14.

The Intergalactic Council

Alariel: Atlantis was a vast spiritual experiment, testing whether human beings could live a physical life and still remain linked to Oneness, also perceived as the Source or the All. This experiment was planned and overseen by the Intergalactic Council, a collaboration of human Master-souls, advanced Star Beings from this galaxy and other galaxies, and a host of angels.

The technical input came mainly from the Star Beings while the monitoring of progress and the system of analysis, summary, and reporting back to the Council was the responsibility of the vast team of angels. Specific aspects were delegated to smaller groups of Council members, and the whole Council only met in formal session at periodic conferences to discuss significant developments and make major decisions. Most of the day-to-day decisions were made at lower levels by angels and Star Beings in implementing the broad policies laid down by the Council.

Although Atlantis as a whole civilization spanned about 240,000 years, the Golden Age only lasted for 1500 years—a key period during which the Atlanteans maintained their connection to Oneness whilst manifesting highly advanced spiritual and technological powers. This perfect blend of the spiritual and the physical was very difficult to maintain. It was a unique state of balance which opened up a whole range of psychic, healing, and consciousness-related powers. We say "unique" because no other civilization on the Earth managed to maintain such a high balance of the physical and the spiritual for such a long period.

The Intergalactic Council were aware of the bigger picture and saw Atlantis as part of a pattern of development that continued the experience of the earlier civilization of Lemuria—a vast continent which covered much of the area now occupied by the Pacific Ocean. The Lemurians were androgynous, and their consciousness focused more at the group than the individual level—but most importantly, they were etheric rather than physical beings. The etheric is the next division of matter above the physical level.

As an etheric being, you would float over the ground rather than treading firmly upon it, and you would not be able to experience the physical senses. That means that the whole area of taste, touch, smell, and sensation would be beyond your reach. The Lemurians became aware of this physical world just beyond their grasp, and they naturally wished to experience it. So the souls who had lived etherically on Lemuria decided to become physical beings on Atlantis where they could access the whole range of human life—the ecstasy and the agony. The approval of the angelic host for this new development was given, and the Intergalactic Council was brought together to plan and oversee the whole operation.

The members of the Council took their responsibilities seriously and tried to set up ideal conditions to make this transition from the etheric to the physical as trouble free as possible. They spent much time briefing the Lemurian souls who had volunteered to take part in the Atlantean experiment before they entered incarnation so that—at the soul level, at least—they were as prepared as possible.

The Intergalactic Council also gathered a limited number of volunteers from other star systems, so that the Lemurian souls would have the benefit of wise guidance and effective mentoring.

And when the terra-forming work to create an appropriate landscape was completed, the great Atlantean experiment was ready to begin.

15.

The Five Phases of Atlantis

Alariel: To understand the development of Atlantean civilization it is necessary to follow its progress through a number of eras or phases. The whole Atlantean period lasted from about 250,000 BCE to about 10,000 BCE, and during this period of time there were five main phases of development:

First Phase: 250,000 BCE - 150,000 BCE
        Destroyed by volcanic activity

Second Phase: 150,000 BCE - 100,000 BCE
        Destroyed by the impact of a giant comet

Third Phase: 100,000 BCE - 52,000 BCE
        Destroyed when the use of anti-matter got out of control

Fourth Phase: 28,000 BCE - 18,000 BCE
        Destroyed by the violent shifting of the Earth's magnetic pole which led to an Ice Age

Fifth Phase: 16,000 BCE - 10,000BCE
        (This includes the Golden Age from about 14,000 BCE to about 12,500 BCE)

Destroyed by the shifting of the tectonic plates which caused major earthquakes and tidal waves.

All these dates are approximate. It should also be borne in mind that there was always a gap—in some cases many thousands of years—between a time of destruction and the establishment of a new civilization for the next phase. Hence, Atlantis was never inhabited during the total span of its existence from 250,000 BCE to the point of its final destruction in about 10,000 BCE. It could, therefore, be more accurately described as five civilizations inhabiting approximately the same area although during the five phases the landmass of Atlantis went through major changes:

First Phase: Atlantis was a giant continent covering most of what is now the Atlantic Ocean.
Second Phase: The landmass had split into many large islands.
Third Phase: The area of ocean had increased, and there were now five large islands.
Fourth Phase: Only the high parts of the five islands survived; the rest of the land was flooded by the ocean.
Fifth Phase: Only one large island remained.

In each of the five phases, the seeding of Atlantis was planned and supervised by the Intergalactic Council. The development of each civilization was closely watched and monitored, but in the case of four of these phases, the experiment had to be terminated by the Council. In the case of the third phase, Atlantis was destroyed by scientific experiments involving the use of anti-matter as a weapon: these experiments got out of control.

It should be understood that when the Council reached decisions to terminate Atlantean civilization four times, these decisions were taken very sadly and reluctantly after examining all the available options. The angels who had overseen the day-to-day monitoring of developments on Atlantis were thorough in investigating possible solutions to the problems as they arose, but in the case of each of the four agreed terminations, these problems had become too severe to be corrected.

During the first two phases of Atlantis, the land was prepared as an earthly paradise before the arrival of the new inhabitants. The angelic host, working with advanced technicians from other star civilizations, manifested ideal buildings and temples so that the incoming souls would have a perfect place for this spiritual experiment. During the first two phases, the new arrivals were mainly Lemurian souls, who were now becoming fully physical for the first time. A small number of advanced teachers from other star systems also came to provide mentoring, wisdom, and inspiration.

However, the descent into physical life and the experience of sex had unforeseen consequences within the first two phases. The Lemurians had come from a subtle and super-physical experience, and when they began to function as individual physical and sexual beings, they found this new experience very difficult. Many were overwhelmed by the intensity of this experience, and the addition of the turbulent emotions of envy and jealousy brought major crises at the level of the psyche. Faced with all these difficulties within an unfamiliar framework of individual choice, many began to slip back into a group experience, something they had known in many lives on Lemuria. Now, however, they had a physical nature to contend with, and this led to many of the Atlanteans using sex as a group process that focused on performance and eliminated love and affection. This shifting of sex from a one-to-one loving relationship to a series of group orgies spread rapidly amongst the Atlantean population and began to develop violent and sadistic elements. When this bestiality became combined with sorcery, it was clear that the Lemurian souls were in danger of devolving rather than evolving spiritually. In these circumstances, the Council reluctantly recognized that termination of the experiment was the only available option for phases One and Two.

For Phase Three, the Intergalactic Council decided to take a different approach. Once more, a pleasant landscape, including houses and temples, was provided, but this time many volunteer souls were invited to come in from other star systems to add to the souls from the original Lemurian group. These new star visitors brought advanced psychic, consciousness-related, and technological abilities, which totally re-invigorated Atlantean culture and provided a new beginning.

For a time, the experiment seemed to go well, but eventually the population of Atlantis split into two groups:

The Wise Ones, who were intelligent, balanced, and loving people who lived in harmony and purity.

The Degenerates, who were lazy, greedy, violent, and sex-obsessed.

There was no real meeting-ground between these two groups, and they came to regard each other with fear and loathing. However, this was not the only major problem that faced the Atlanteans of the Third Phase. The natural cycle of the evolutionary process produced over time large numbers of giant animals. This was partly the result of creating an ideal landscape without natural predators who would keep any given species within some bounds of control. The landscape had been made perfect for the humans, but in doing this, the process of animal evolution had been compromised.

Another development that had not been foreseen made the whole situation more complex. These giant animals began to respond to the violent feelings within the consciousness of the Degenerate group. This changed their natural pattern of behavior, and the animals became increasingly ferocious and aggressive.

Attempts were made to fence in and control the giant animals, but these efforts were undermined by sabotage on the part of the Degenerates, who felt sympathy for these animals and saw them in some ill-defined way as possible allies in their struggle against the Wise Ones. After many desperate attempts to pen in the giant animals had failed, the Atlantean scientists, who by this time had benefited greatly from the advanced technical skills of the starseeds, came up with a bold solution. They had already been experimenting for some time with the interface between matter and anti-matter. Now they proposed to develop this technology into a weapon and use it against the giant animals.

However, anti-matter technology is notoriously difficult to control, which is why many star systems have banned it. Although the Atlantean scientists did manage to kill the giant animals, the experiment ran out of control, causing massive earthquakes and tidal waves which destroyed all human life. The Earth shifted on its axis, and Atlantis became five large islands, the remaining land being engulfed by the ocean.

Then in 28,000 BCE the Intergalactic Council met and decided to reseed Atlantis for a fourth Phase. Now only the higher parts of the five islands remained with the rest of the original landmass being flooded by the ocean. This time most of the Lemurian souls from previous phases were transferred to other star systems where they could be guided and mentored more effectively. The small number of Lemurian souls who volunteered to return to Atlantis were accompanied by large numbers of visitors from other star systems.

The Fourth Phase was to be set up on an entirely different basis. The incoming souls were given a pleasant landscape but no buildings, and the need to work together in the construction of houses and temples bonded the new Atlanteans together for a time.

However, eventually the same split emerged between Wise Ones and Degenerates, and a mixture of technology and sorcery was used to control people. Chaos replaced order, and Atlantis slipped into a long cycle of criminality, violence, and war. Once again, the Council decided to terminate the experiment. In 18,000 BCE the violent shifting of the Earth's magnetic pole led to an abrupt change in climate and the onset of an Ice Age.

When the Intergalactic Council met to consider a Fifth Phase of the Atlantean experiment, they settled upon a very different structure with much greater supervision and control. Working through twelve advanced Beings (collectively called the Alta) they set up the new Atlantis in twelve regions. Each region was governed by a High Priest or Priestess who was one of the Alta with sweeping powers and the backing of an effective administrative structure.

Once more, volunteers came in from several galaxies, but this time only water, earth, and plant life were provided. As this meant a more extended period of cooperation was needed, the experiment got off to a better start. Eventually a Golden Age of high spiritual and technical excellence emerged—a period that still stands as the high peak of human achievement.

Sadly the period of Golden Atlantis could not be sustained forever. Gradually selfishness, greed, lust, and overwork crept into Atlantean life and overwhelmed most of the people. The followers of the Wise Ones who maintained the knowledge that they were Children of the Light tried to warn the rest of the people, but they were laughed at and scorned. A twisted society of shallow celebrity, selfish exploitation, and violent criminality emerged, working hand in hand with a very advanced technology that dehumanized people.

Animals were over-worked and exploited, and then new creatures—half-human and half-animal—were created through advanced genetic science. These mutants alarmed the angels monitoring Atlantean society more than any other development. An angel has an acute awareness of how physical beings fit into the structure of Creation with regard to the soul. Angels know that all animals have a group-soul with an angelic being responsible for its oversight. When an animal through self-sacrifice or continued contact with humans is able to graduate beyond this group-soul, a new human soul is created. This pattern—animals with group-souls, humans with individual souls—is an immutable law throughout the angelic world.

But now angels were confronted with new creatures that were neither entirely animal nor entirely human. Should these mutants be given human souls or not? A deep level of alarm swept through the angelic host whilst down on Atlantis, chaos was engulfing the land.

The mutants, half-animal and half-human, were spreading increasingly complex and virulent forms of disease that had never been seen before and for which even the skilled medical scientists of Atlantis had no answer. Meanwhile, the whole of Atlantean society was already sick for other reasons. The water had become polluted, and health was declining everywhere. Life for many Atlanteans had become a grim process of overwork, exploitation, inadequate rest, and heavy food. In these harsh conditions, alcohol and drug abuse became more and more common. People sleep-walked through their lives and forgot the feeling of love and the meaning of joy. Science and a hard, unforgiving technology dominated life, and creativity and spirituality were squeezed out. As Atlantis went into its final decline, illness, violence, and criminality dominated the society.

In addition to these problems, the ever more bold and reckless Atlantean scientists were abusing crystal technology by developing enormous crystals as part of their energy program. Once a crystal reaches a certain size, its power increases dramatically, and the Atlantean scientists had not mastered the techniques for controlling these crystals. Worse still, they were beginning to experiment with a process for drawing power from the molten core of the Earth—a technology so dangerous that, should it be allowed to continue, it would almost certainly have destroyed the whole planet.

Given these imminent dangers, the widespread chaos and breakdown of civilized life, and the firm objections from the angelic host on the mutant issue, the Intergalactic Council had no alternative. Atlantis had to be terminated, and the great experiment abandoned forever. In 10,000 BCE the tectonic plates shifted, and the Atlantean landmass fragmented and crumbled down into a vast mass of mud which would form a maritime hazard for many years to come.

The final phase of Atlantis was over, and the golden dream of the highest and most spiritual civilization this world has ever known was now becoming a legend, a distant folk-memory in the history of the human race.

16.

Atlantis in Perspective

Alariel: When one sees only the outline of the Atlantean experiment—five phases and five abrupt terminations—it must inevitably seem like an elaborate failure. But if you look more deeply into the reasons for termination, and the difficulties that had to be overcome, a different picture starts to emerge.

From the very beginning Atlantis had to deal with a very challenging situation. At the start of the experiment, the vast bulk of the incoming souls were relatively "young" souls with a limited experience, that experience being confined to etheric lives on the continent of Lemuria. None of these Lemurian lives would have prepared them for the very different experience on Atlantis.

Here for the first time, these young and inexperienced souls became fully physical and were faced with the whole gamut of physical sensation and the broad range of human emotions, including guilt, shame, hurt and fear. This was so painful and confusing to souls who had floated through much gentler super-physical lives within a group focus that many of them retreated into another form of group experience— the group experience of sex. However, this was a slippery path that led to spiritual devolution. It locked them into a process which steadily reduced their vibrational rate until they began resonating at subhuman levels.

It was this process of degeneration into bestiality than led to the termination of the first two phases, but Phases Three and Four also faced major challenges. The influx of large numbers of advanced star beings from across this and other galaxies transformed Atlantean technology, but it also intensified the split in Atlantean society, which polarized into the high vibration Wise Ones and the primitive Degenerates. And the Atlantean scientists, freed from the caution born of long experience on their original star systems, began to develop their technology into increasingly dangerous areas.

The fifth and final phase tried to correct the previous imbalances by setting up a structure with much firmer leadership and control. Under the guidance of twelve advanced Beings, this system did produce harmony and stability for a time, culminating in the Golden Age of Atlantis. Yet even here the seeds of destruction were contained in the fabric of Atlantean society. These very advanced technologies began to dehumanize the population, which led in time to a split between the exploiters of this technology and those exploited by it. Pride in advanced scientific skills, combined with ruthless greed, led to the extensive abuse of the animal kingdom. That abuse reached its peak in the development of mutant forms, half-human and half-animal. And so the stage was set for the final termination of the whole Atlantean experiment.

In coming to a final assessment of this great experiment, the individual good has to be weighed in the balance, alongside the evident failures of Atlantean society as a whole. On Atlantis many souls experienced their most intense, creative, harmonious, and spiritual lives which then contributed greatly to their soul growth. The era of Golden Atlantis continues to stand as humanity's greatest spiritual achievement and an inspiration to many souls who are now reaching up again towards the very highest frequencies of Light and Love.

And when the Atlantean period was finally over, the knowledge was not lost. Well before the time of the final destruction, the great Teachers of the final phase took their followers by ship to new locations across the globe. There they worked to seed the wisdom of Atlantis into new civilizations who would take the human story forward within a number of unique traditions.

The Atlantean legacy remains a potent force in human development because Atlantis is still an inspiration within the New Consciousness. Thus, the spiritual harvest of Atlantis continues to serve humanity in its long pilgrimage, a pilgrimage which is now set to reach its climax in the Transition of the Earth and the Triumph of the Light.

Part Five:

A Time of Transformation

17.

The Context of 2012

Alariel: In the whole of the Mayan Calendar, the twenty-five years from 1987 to 2012 are identified as the time of most rapid change. During this period the processes of linear time steadily accelerate in an arc of transformation that lifts humanity out of a veiled semi-sleep state into a conscious level of awakening. In a sense all have been experiencing a period of dreaming that separated them from the main dynamic of the universe, and now all are rejoining the Universe again.

This dream has had a cyclical, repeating pattern to it, and within it change only came slowly. But now that all are awakening, all begin to see that nothing is really static in the Universe. Every part of life is changing, developing, and moving on to another form or another level of experience. For the truth is that change is found everywhere, and any attempt to hold back that change, any clinging to a fixed position, a rigid attitude, an immovable perception, will eventually be swept away by the natural process of the universal life-force.

There is also a much bigger context for 2012: the whole galaxy is rising in vibration, ascending into the Light and returning to Source. This is a major shift in emphasis within all creation as God stops moving outwards and down into matter and starts moving inwards and up into the Light. The whole pattern of activity within the universe is beginning to reflect this shift, and the changes all are experiencing on the Earth need to be seen as part of this bigger picture. The time has come for individual ascension, planetary ascension, and galactic ascension into a higher and subtler state of being. Given a context as vast as this, the shift into a New Consciousness and a New World takes on a different meaning.

This is the context within which all the processes of change at the personal and planetary levels occur. An understanding of this framework prepares the ground for a consideration of the Principles of Transformation and the detailed working out of the whole 2012 Experience. And that Experience prepares the way for a new perception of God.

Once you start to expand your awareness and think about God as the aggregate of universal consciousness, many other things fall into place. For example, you will begin to understand why God is not exempt from the pattern of change. If you think of God as the aggregate consciousness of all the consciousnesses in the universe, then it becomes clear that as all beings learn and grow and develop, so God must change and develop, too. A changing web of sentient beings and an unchanging God would simply be incompatible. But there is a vast mystery involved here: in a sense change is *one of the few underlying constants in the universe.* Perceptions alter, values evolve, consciousness expands, but change is seen at every level of development, and the one thing you can always rely upon is the constancy of change. It is this constancy that human beings as their newly-awakened Selves are beginning to see for the first time. And it is change that challenges all sentient beings to trust the process and let go of everything in their lives which is heavy, rigid, and fixed.

Comment by Stuart: Inspired by this last section I wrote the following poem:

> The mystery of mysteries
> is the constancy of change,
> and if we try to hold on,
> then life will rearrange
> all our fixed positions
> and all our sacred cows
> until we learn to let go
> of all our rigid vows.

18.

Some Principles of Transformation

Alariel: You are currently caught up in a vortex of change so intense that at times you can scarcely catch your breath, and it is helpful at this point to know that you are supported and guided by the angelic realm more intensively than ever before. We know how much this rapid and accelerating process of change is demanding of you, and we are committed to giving you total support. Extensive help is now available; however, remember that to receive the maximum benefit from it, you do need to ask for help! No one is expected to struggle on alone, and the more you are open to guidance, help and healing, the more support you will receive as you evolve towards the Light.

This evolution towards higher levels of consciousness is built into every sentient being, and your present awakening is simply a reflection of this. The arc of human spiritual evolution is vast beyond your understanding although a few principles may help to clarify this:

1. Light is the key symbol of transformation, and the heart is the focal point in the process of change.
2. When you expand your consciousness, you become open to options that go far beyond anything that you can now imagine.

3. It is important to know who you've been in order to understand who you are. It is equally important to let go of the drama of your past lives and focus on being here now.

4. As you move into the 2012 experience, the need to resolve past life energies will steadily be replaced by the need to reconnect with the soul and activate the heart.

5. No experience in this or any other life is good or bad in itself. The toughest lessons can provide the best opportunities to learn and grow.

6. You have traveled upon many journeys across the face of this planet but the most important journey is the journey within.

7. As your consciousness expands, your perception of God will evolve and expand, too. These perceptions will become more universal, more subtle, and more transpersonal.

8. The steady progress of planetary systems towards the Light has been marked by a few moments of massive breakthrough: the Transition of the Earth in 2012 is one of these moments.

9. Spiritual teaching and mentoring on this planet has not been a series of solo performances but a vast team effort, involving initiates, aspirants, angels, and star beings.

10. As you evolve, the differences between human beings, star beings, and angelic beings will steadily diminish. As the streams of life progress, they naturally converge.

11. All sentient beings in the universe evolve towards the ultimate level of the Elohim. Wherever you start, this is the fullest flowering of consciousness.

12. Spirit transcends the normal functioning of space and time. The more you enter the level of Spirit, the more multidimensional you become.

19.

The 2012 Experience

Joanna: Although we are moving into many new things at this time of change, there seems to be a return of old wisdom, old skills and many good things that we have forgotten from the past. Could you comment on this please?

Alariel: The paradox of the New Consciousness is that it will enable many human beings to reach levels of awareness that were last seen many centuries ago in Atlantis. Atlantis is valuable to you as an inspiration: the significance of Golden Atlantis is its ability to inspire many people to rise to their highest levels of being and consciousness. These levels have been out of reach for a long time now, but they will soon become a routine part of your lives.

As you move into the 2012 Experience, many things will become possible for you that were inaccessible before the planetary energies started to change and the Earth began to move into its transition to the fifth dimensional (or 5D) reality. The 5D experience is going to be dramatically different to the third dimensional (or 3D) experience of your current world and will involve a vibrational shift, which will lift and realign your consciousness.

This will be a big shift for humanity, but in times of crisis you demonstrate that you're already moving beyond the old greed-and-competition scenario. In theory you may regard all other countries as your economic competitors, but when a natural disaster hits any area of your planet, you abandon the principles of a competitive economy. Instead of rejoicing in the misfortunes of your competitors, you pour money and resources on a global scale into helping those in the disaster area.

What you can do now only at times of crisis, you will soon be able to achieve all the time. To help you make this major breakthrough in consciousness your planet is receiving practical assistance in the form of the advanced beings now being born, as Indigos give way to Crystal Children and eventually to the Rainbow Children. Together these Masters of the Technology of Light and Love will transform your consciousness and help you to move on and achieve your full potential. A few principles may serve to highlight that potential:

1. Humans are multidimensional and meta-gifted beings who are starting to step into their power and expand their consciousness.
2. As your horizons expand, your ability to heal and to heal others increases greatly.
3. When your consciousness expands, your vibration rises, your DNA changes, and your chakras start to unify.
4. When the chakras unify, you become the crucible within which spiritual transformation can occur.
5. This process of transformation leads naturally to enlightenment and ascension. Ascension is stepping into the next dimensional reality in order to access further levels of spiritual growth. Ascension is made possible by an awakening of Love in the heart.

6. The whole of creation is moving upwards into Unity. Having explored separateness and density, the universe is ascending into Light and returning to Source.

7. What is important about 2012 is not a single date but the whole of the 2012 experience. This will be a gateway into a New World and a New Consciousness.

   As you move through the whole of this transformative 2012 Experience, healing occurs at the most profound level as the oneness of the individual begins to reflect the Oneness of all life. The journey of the individual parallels the whole pattern of creation as individuals, planets, solar systems, and galaxies rise upwards into the Light.

Comment by Stuart: Armed with a whole raft of interesting questions she had been developing, our friend Catherine Mary La Toure came for a session with Alariel during March 2009. Her questions focused on 2012 and its implications.

Catherine Mary: Are *we* really *going to have things happening in 2012?*

Alariel: Things will happen, but how you perceive the changes depends upon the frequency of your consciousness. Everyone will notice some changes, of course, but those whose consciousness is deeply rooted in conventional life will see only conventional changes: the earthquakes and the crumbling of the social fabric.

   The people with a much higher frequency of consciousness will see remarkable and positive things happening. You've already begun to notice the extraordinary skills and powers that are emerging, but these things will not be perceptible to the average people in the street. They will expect simple and down-to-earth things to happen, and, indeed, these things will be happening, too.

As the 2012 Experience progresses, the awareness of living in a multidimensional universe will steadily grow. Many people will feel drawn to enquire about dimensional realities, and a much clearer understanding will gradually emerge.

We perceive the fourth dimension as the Interlife, the space between lives, the frequency of vibration you experience when you pass over. It's very easy to get into 4D: it occurs automatically when you die. Getting into 5D—the fifth dimension—is different because it involves an ascension process. The fifth dimensional reality provides a platform for the ongoing development of beings capable of much higher forms of consciousness. So it's a complete world of experience.

If you have a 3D reality, and you have experience at the physical level, then you've got to have somewhere to go when you pass over and you're not in physical form any more. There has to be a 'waiting room' before the next incarnation and that is the fourth dimension. Some people call it the Afterlife, the Interlife, the Summerlands. It doesn't matter what you call it, but it's a necessary part of the process of having a physical existence. Because if you are physical here, you're only physical for a time, and then you need somewhere to withdraw and consult your angelic advisors about your plans for the next life.

Now when you go on to 5D, there isn't a question of withdrawal because you will be there permanently until you move upwards into higher dimensional levels.

Joanna: *Didn't we come from the fifth dimension originally anyway?*

A: Correct. If you go back far enough in time, then you began as sparks from the One Flame which exists at the highest dimensional level. But over great eons of time, you have been moving down into much denser levels: you've been working through the closed loop of 3D and 4D experience, but there are many dimensions beyond that.

C: *Are we all going into the fifth dimension or do we have a choice? Do we still have things to do here?*

A: You only ascend when your self-appointed task, your mission on Earth, is completed. We can't tell you exactly when that will be because that's up to you to decide when you've completed it! Your higher self will decide when the job is done. The timing is entirely in your hands.

C: *So might we eventually—or anyway some of us—end up doing another 26,000 years in the third dimension?*

A: People who are radically resistant to change, who are into denial in a big way and/or who want to stay locked at the ego-dominated level will require a physical, 3D environment to do that in. The people who wish to continue with war, conflict, and heavy density activities can continue to do that, but they will have to do it on another planet because the Earth will not allow that. When she goes through her Transition, Earth will be a perfect home for fifth dimensional beings but a very uncomfortable place for third dimensional beings. However, there is a nice 3D planet being prepared for them by the angelic host. Preparations for Earth Mark Two have been well-advanced for a long time now.

J: *I see so many incredible things happening, and because of my interacting with people, it is just amazing what is going on now. It's been a big wake-up call for us with people communicating about our books from all over the world.*

A: Indeed, but opportunities will occur at various times and at various levels. Some people will wait until it is very late in the process when there's a great wave of awakening. The thing you have to bear in mind is that the people who are awake—really awake—are relatively few. They're increasing in numbers all the time, but they are still relatively few compared with total world population. What will happen as you move towards 2012 is like a series of waves and more and more people wake up. And as the numbers increase, the ability of these awake people to influence others and wake up those around them will increase, too.

As the waves of Light pulsate over the planet with increasing speed, what will happen is that even the "resisters" and "denyers" will feel some influence as all approach the time of transition. So there will be an opportunity for everyone to wake up. The best possible scenario is that all human beings wake up. They may be carried along by the energies of all those people around them waking up and coming into their power, and a realization of their real nature as Children of the Light. For example, if all the other members of your family wake up, how are you NOT going to wake up? It will be very hard for anyone to resist at that point!

C: *Suppose my sister has had other lives, but in this one she chose to be a not very pleasant person, could she ascend because of all the other lives when she was a more enlightened person?*

A: You ascend as the totality of your being, focused at a certain level of consciousness now. Some people may have slipped back in a sense, but it's what levels they've reached in aggregate and where they are now. And that's a balance.

J: *So it's really hard to tell where people are, what level they have reached?*

A: All we can advise you to do is suspend judgment totally. You really can't tell by looking at a human being whether they are going to ascend or not. It's to do with the waves of Light accelerating across Earth. Sometimes the heart can be remarkably closed for a long time, but it just receives a certain pulse of energy from Spirit and it's like a flower opening, and the person makes enormous strides in a matter of seconds.

Time is not important here. People can do it in a matter of seconds—going from a closed-down, crabby state to an advanced being when all the blocks and limitations fall away, and the real Self shines through. Transition is going to be a massive shockwave of change, and it will affect different people in different ways all over the planet.

C: *Even though it's coming up so soon now?*

A: You're thinking in linear terms whereas the Transition is trans-linear and trans-dimensional. When we talk about these waves of Light, what we're really talking about is incoming pulses of the Spirit. The Spirit is beyond time, beyond space, and beyond dimension—in fact, it is beyond all the limitations implied in those three things. When the Spirit moves, time disappears, and the miraculous becomes possible. And that involves a transcending, a going beyond all of the laws of physics as you know them. If you want to call that magic, then it is a kind of magic.

When the Spirit moves, magic enters your life, and the whole area of planetary transition and the ascension of humanity can be seen as the High Magic, the intervention of Grace to take you from your present level into much greater opportunities for learning and spiritual growth. And the possibility is opening up for you to move into 5D from a point of awareness in your present lives.

C: *Are there some people who have already died and will simply transfer from the fourth to the fifth dimension?*

A: Yes, you can also go from 4D to 5D. When a planet goes into transition, it's a point of decision for the planet, but it's also a point of decision for individual human beings. You'll be given the choice of doing whatever work you wish to do. If you want to stay here and serve, that's fine. And if you want to go somewhere else in the galaxy, that's also fine, but if you choose to do that, you'll go into Light and simply vanish from the perspective of those people around you at that time.

C: *So some people will suddenly disappear?*

A: Yes, those who have chosen to serve elsewhere. Of course, it is hoped that many will wish to stay here. It's going to be a much better environment than you've had in the past.

C: *But if people choose to stay in the third dimension, and, therefore, they're not going to stay with the Earth, will they simply die?*

A: Yes. They will go through the normal Interlife experience, and then they will be born on the next 3D planet, having no memory at all of planet Earth. They'll just be born as children on Earth Mark Two and think what a wonderful place that is and pursue all their ego games for as many thousand years as they wish until they reach their own ascension process. And at that point you may volunteer to go to that planet to teach them, and they may ask, "How is it that you became such wonderful Beings of Light?" And you may reply, "Well, we were on a planet called Earth with you, but you chose one path and we chose another."

J: *What some writers are saying is that to a conventional person, it may look as if people are vanishing and you can't see them anymore, but ascension is a question of dimensional frequency. If the people who vanish are on a different frequency, you just can't see them, even if they are standing right there next to you.*

A: That is true. This room might be full of fifth dimensional beings but you wouldn't see them. Basically, you can't see the next dimension up, the next complete world of experience, using the normal sight of this current world.

If you have beyond-the-normal sight, like psychic vision, you can see them, but with normal vision you can't see your ancestors who are in 4D even if they were here in this room.

J: *But I know so many people who have seen manifestations of Jeshua and other Masters.*

A: But that's because they have had a glimmering of exceptional sight for a short time.

J: *And there are more and more people who are walking with angels.*

A: Agreed. The veil is starting to thin as the planet nears transition.

C: *If you're in the fifth dimension, you see dead people, or people in the Interlife who have just died?*

A: Basically, you can look down and see any lower dimensional world. So if you're a 5D being, you can look down and see 4D or 3D.

C: *After transition will the Law of Free Will still apply?*

A: Yes, but it is free will within a greater context. What really happens when you go into transition is you move from the ego-dominated personality level fully into the soul level. Now if you've been contacting higher levels of your consciousness, you have been trying to live the life of the soul as best you can, but most people are still influenced by the ego to some degree. To be *totally* beyond the ego is quite an advanced stage. So after transition you will get more and more into the process of living the life of the soul. And the ego-driven side of the personality will simply fade away; it will become almost like a dream to you, as you feel it fade away. You won't want to live at the ego level anymore; you'll think much more of the greater good of all concerned and much less of the needs and wishes of the personality.

C: *Is that what it is like for Ascended Masters like St. Germain?*

A: Oh yes, and it has been like that for some time. All Ascended Masters are able to put the good of humanity and the greater good extended over a long timeframe way ahead of their own personal wishes. However, they don't take this process to extremes so that their physical health breaks down because while they remain physical beings, it is still a balance for them, and they have to maintain effective physical function. They love their neighbor as themselves but still love themselves so that they can continue to serve their neighbor.

        If you cease to love yourself, then your ability to serve your neighbors diminishes through ill-health and ceases altogether when you don't have a physical body.

C: *How would you advise us to prepare for moving into the fifth dimension?*

A: We have already communicated a whole raft of practical advice in another book, and so we would refer you to that.

Comment by Stuart: The reference here to "another book" is to the third book we published with Ozark Mountain Publishing: it is called *Beyond Limitations: The Power of Conscious Co-Creation.* The chapter on 'Personal and Planetary Changes' is relevant here, and there is a series of ten practical steps in 'Transition and the Big Questions' which readers may find useful in preparation for the transition.

The session with Alariel continues.

J: *Do you have any general comments on 2012 and the transition?*

A: 2012 is really a journey into the energy and wisdom of the heart. You have explored the world of the senses and the world of the mind. Now it is time to explore the Way of the Heart.

This is an exciting time to be alive—the period of greatest change and greatest opportunity in any planet's development when it goes into transition from one dimensional reality to the next. And you're alive, here and now, and able to make a difference. Isn't that wonderful timing? We congratulate you on your perfect timing!

Comment by Stuart: This had been a highly productive session, and we are most grateful to Catherine Mary for researching and compiling such an interesting list of questions to cover this area so thoroughly.

Part Six:

Towards the
New Consciousness

20.

The Dynamics of Healing

Joanna: Is change a key factor in the healing process?
Alariel: Oh yes. And the implications of this are only just now
being perceived on your planet. It is only by seeing
change as the core of the healing process that you can
begin to understand what healing really is.

Healing is fundamentally a process of moving into
resolution—that is, resolution in the way a musician
understands this term: the release of drama and tension
experienced when passing through discord and the
restoration of concord. This can also be described as the
transition from conflict to harmony. This perception is
deeply symbolic: a transition upwards in vibration
involving a passing from conflict into harmony is
exactly what your planet, your solar system and your
galaxy are now beginning to experience. All these
elements are moving upwards out of shadowplay and
into the Light.

Certain principles underlie this process and may
help to clarify the dynamics of harmony:

1. Whereas harmony is a stable state, discord is
   essentially unstable;
2. While concordant systems can continue with little
   energy to sustain them, discordant systems require a

disproportionate amount of energy to maintain them.

3. Resolution of a discordant state opens the door to change, healing, and spiritual growth.

Your society has become obsessed with the persona, the mask that you wear, and your story locks you into that mask. Releasing the story initiates the process of change, and, as the mask begins to fall away, a reconnection with your real Self starts to pull you out of time and into timeless possibilities.

As long as the story rolls on, you are locked energetically into your role, a single viewpoint, and a fixed strand in the storyline—and all the drama which flows from that. Let go of the story, release the drama, and that energy dissolves and disappears. Then there is only YOU, only your consciousness and being, and at last you can see things as they really are.

> When the play is over,
> what you get is reality.

The drama locks you into time; when you let the drama go, you rediscover your real nature as a timeless multidimensional Being of Light.

> If you want the Truth,
> you have to get beyond the story.
> If you want the Light,
> you have to get beyond the shadowplay.
> If you want Healing,
> you have to get beyond the drama.

Comment by Stuart: It is fascinating how much of this channeling mirrors the work being done by Philippa Merivale in the development of a remarkable system called Metatronic

Healing. In her *Foundation Course Workbook*, Metatronic Healing is described as a method that enables you to transcend the 'stories' or the myths that have directed your life in the past and move to a higher level of truth:

> As long as we are weighed down by our history, our herstory, carrying in our bodies the burdens of the grief and anger and frustration and hopelessness and jealousy and regret and all the other stuff that goes with that history, of course, we can't lighten up.

Comment by Stuart: On the second day of December 2009, I channeled Alariel and received this information about Metatronic Healing.

A: Do not confuse Metatronic Healing with any of the new healing modalities which are now emerging, for it has a much vaster potential. As this system develops, it will become what I can only describe as the Yoga of the New Age. This Yoga unites you with your hidden Wholeness. It is needed now if human beings are to move beyond their time-related drama and into a reconnection with their timeless Selves as Children of the Light.

    The Yoga of the New Age will involve the unrolling of a Language of Light which is still only on the fringes of what you can presently perceive, and that unrolling will prepare the way for many wonderful possibilities. If you think of this Language as a higher frequency of music, you will begin to glimpse its power and quality.

Comment by Stuart: When we asked Alariel to comment on the need to lighten up, this was his response:

A: Your planet has become a battleground between the heavy and the light, and you need to make a choice in many areas of your life. We suggest you say to yourself:

> I choose the Light
> and the Ways of Light.
> All that is heavy
> falls away from me now.

You are being challenged to find lighter ways of living, and this applies in many areas, including traditions, values, relationships, social customs, diet and work patterns. Your society has become far too rigid, combative and driven by greed, fear, and security issues. All of these things are profoundly heavy, and both individually and as a society you need to lighten up. And above all, you need to learn to live lightly on the Earth.

Perhaps a few Principles of Lightness may be useful here:

1. Skim lightly over the waves of life: do not thump into them like an overloaded ship.
2. Lightness enables you to see more possibilities and more options.
3. Faced with two options, always choose the lighter one.
4. Lightness leads to increased creativity and greater balance.
5. Don't get pulled into the heavy stories of those around you: let them deal with their own karma-drama.
6. The ancient hobnailed boots of tradition are too heavy for today: what you need now are light and agile dancing shoes.

7. When life becomes a song to be danced and a dance to be sung, you'll know you've got it right!

21.

The New Consciousness

Alariel: We appreciate that there is a lot of focus now upon the 2012 experience, but from our perspective what is really important is the New Consciousness. Long after 2012 disappears into distant memory, the New Consciousness will form a significant part of human development.

It is very difficult to describe the soon-to-emerge developments in your consciousness while staying within your present vocabulary. As your consciousness changes, you vocabulary will evolve to keep pace with it. This is illustrated by several principles that underlie the development of the new consciousness:

Your consciousness is beginning to frequence upwards into new modalities.

To 'frequence' your consciousness is to uplift its frequency in a series of wave-like modulations. Initially, your consciousness cannot settle at the higher level but simply visits it, but with each upward wave the ability to hold the higher frequency increases.

Your consciousness moves upwards in a series of pulses that lift its vibrational frequency. These pulses are like waves, and they lift the frequency of your consciousness into progressively higher levels, the waves rising up and then falling back but continuing over time the upwards movement. This upliftment of the vibrational frequency of your consciousness gives you access to new modalities of being (new ways in which your consciousness can function) that involve new skills, new levels of awareness, and a whole new vocabulary in which to express these new experiences.

Over time people who experience and communicate these new modalities will evolve a whole new language, a language that will become a vehicle both of expression and transformation. Do not imagine that only the very young will be able to speak and use this language. Yes, the Crystal Children will be adept at using it, but souls who have retired from the intense activities of life and continue to develop their consciousness and hone their sensitivity will also have a unique opportunity over the next few years to explore this new language.

When a human being becomes elderly, he or she either moves downwards into greater materialism (and selfishness) or upwards into greater sensitivity (and universality.) The sensitivity route is a gateway to a much wider spectrum of experience and consciousness than human beings have enjoyed in the past. These super-sensitive elderly pioneers, together with the Crystal Children who are now being born, and the Rainbow Children who are soon to emerge will push human awareness into exciting and fruitful new areas that can only be called a revolution in consciousness.

You have experienced an industrial revolution, a political revolution, and a communications revolution. All these were preludes to the main event in human development—the Revolution in Consciousness. The previous revolutions took you into developments of your existing world. They changed your working methods, social structures, and interaction processes. Though these changes were major ones, an intelligent person could have predicted many of the outcomes while these revolutions were still in their infancy. The Consciousness Revolution is not like that; we doubt whether any human being now living on the Earth could predict the full extent of the changes that the Consciousness Revolution will bring.

The triple harmonics of expanding consciousness, transforming DNA, and rising vibration; modulate upward in a linked progression.

The way that consciousness, DNA, and vibration, move upwards as one integrated whole is similar to the process of modulation through musical keys. Because these three elements remain linked together, advances in consciousness are always reflected in parallel changes within DNA and vibration. This is the way the integrity of the whole human being is maintained within what is essentially a holistic system, even though that system is moving through a vortex of change.

Individual acceleration of consciousness leads to an acceleration in the whole of human evolution.

Human evolution, which proceeded at a slow pace for centuries, is about to accelerate in a way that few people could have imagined. This rapid development will open up new areas of processing, vocabulary, and language as those going through this evolutionary spiral attempt to communicate the basis of their experiences.

The process of developing machines, however sophisticated, can take you only a few steps along the long road of human potential. If you wish to take giant leaps along that road, you should start looking within at human consciousness and not outwards through the use of machine-based technology.

A combination of expanding human consciousness and the Technology of Light will open up new frequencies of multidimensional experience and new abilities that will reveal your true nature as meta-gifted Beings of Light.

You will discover that human consciousness and the Technology of Light have enormous potential to empower you as multidimensional beings, whereas through machine-based technology you can never be fully empowered or fully free.

The effect of Light within the consciousness and Unconditional Love within the heart, leads to a full activation of the Light Body.

The Light Body is essentially the vehicle of ascension. However, many Light-Workers have a Light Body that is not yet fully activated. The Light Body is activated most effectively through focusing the energy of Unconditional Love through the heart. This needs to be Love both for others and for *oneself*—and this is a balance that some may find difficult. When you move through this activation process, you will be experiencing exactly the process that Jeshua was trying to teach. This process is a far more powerful bringer of change than any rigid intellectual system or traditional religious practice.

The Light Body activation causes pulses of Light which expand the consciousness and integrate the system of force-centers in the body into a new continuum of expanded Being.

When the Light Body is activated, it sends a series of Light pulses into the personality to clarify and integrate the whole system of chakras or force-centers, uplifting and reattuning this system so that is becomes a platform for expanding consciousness and rapid spiritual growth.

When it is fully absorbed and integrated into the whole being right down to the cellular level, this activation leads to the beginning of an ascension process that will open access to further levels of spiritual growth.

Ascension is now being seen in scientific rather than a religious context. This will make it increasingly more acceptable to modern minds who think in terms of a multidimensional universe.

Ascension shifts the focus permanently into the next dimensional reality. This does not necessarily mean leaving the Earth, but it does mean entering a new level of empowerment and a fresh commitment to a life of loving service.

As the Earth has already risen so much in vibration, the option of staying here to serve in an ascended state has now become available. This is a very different situation to that of two thousand years ago when full ascension inevitably meant disappearing into Light and leaving the Earth's frequency since that frequency was so dense and so far from the vibration of the ascended state of being.

However, this whole transition upwards into the Light needs to be put into the greater context of Earth's place in the universe. You are not alone in your efforts to move upwards into the Light, and this is demonstrated by the presence on your planet at this time of so many Indigo, Crystal and Rainbow Children. Their presence here, which is essentially a gift from other star civilizations and other galaxies, underlines the Brotherhood/Sisterhood of all Sentient Beings. You are not alone in moving upwards into the Light, and at this vital time you need—and are receiving—vast amounts of help. This will assist you in moving beyond conflict based on divisions and into a new understanding of what you all share.

All physical sentient beings share in the Divine Image—the mathematical and geometrical basis on which your forms are created. The mathematics and geometry provide the template upon which the angelic host creates the architecture of form for sentient beings throughout the Universe.

Wherever you go in the universe, the underlying foundation of mathematics and geometry connects the whole structure into a single holistic unity. But there is a still deeper unifying element, and that is the foundational Energy of Unconditional Love. It was Love that brought the Universe into being, and Love which sustains it and provides the impetus for change within the consciousness of sentient beings. Whatever spiritual path you choose, the transformative energy of Unconditional Love is there to support and nourish that path and carry through the process of change and transformation within the heart. Simply attuning to this Energy and invoking it within the heart, will begin this process of profound change.

The Energy of Love
is a powerful and transformative force
within many traditions:
it unites every faith and philosophy,
every benevolent impulse
and every random act of kindness.
You do not need
    to go to the mountain top to find it—
it shines in the eyes of all those
who have glimpsed the power of joy
and the ability of love to bless,
    to heal, and to inspire.

When you consider the power of Love working together with the vast resources of the Technology of Light, you begin to glimpse the whole arc of the scheme of spiritual evolution. What we're really talking about here is the power of the Spirit.

If you define magic as a process that transcends the laws of physics, then as the Spirit is certainly capable of transcending those laws, its functioning can be seen as essentially magical. When the Spirit moves, it moves in such a multidimensional way that 3D space and linear time are transcended, and anything is possible. The Spirit links together all beings and transcends all the dimensions of space and frequencies of time. Spirit transcends all of that and affirms Oneness of Life, Oneness of Being, Oneness of Essence.

This is the High Magic that challenges you to set aside your limitations and enter the reality of your multidimensional Being. Because your experience on Earth has diminished you for so long, it's going to be challenging for you to expand into an awareness of the great Beings of Light that you really are, but that is what 2012 and the New Consciousness is moving you towards.

Now is the time to let go of your fears and limitations and enter your full empowerment.

Now is the time to recognize your brothers and sisters who have walked this path with you and given you their love and their friendship.

Now is the time to awaken to who you really are and step forward into your destiny as multidimensional and meta-gifted Beings.

Now is the time to stand up in Love and Power, and let your Light shine.

22.

The Journey to the All

Alariel: Many are now beginning to realize that the 2012
experience is only one stage in the unfolding of your
multidimensional awareness. As you move into that
awareness, you will find that the levels of separation
and division fall way, and you will enter a state of
consciousness where you see things from the standpoint
of complete Oneness. When Jeshua said that Mary
Magdalene was 'The woman who understands the All,'
this was what he meant—an understanding and
knowing and living at the level where there is simply
One Energy and One Consciousness uniting all that is.
And that Energy, that Consciousness, is Unconditional
Love.

When you look at things from the level of the All,
this lifts you above judging, choosing, criticizing, and
taking sides. From this perspective all aspects of
experience are valued equally within the Totality of
Being. This Totality involves functioning right across
what we might call the PEMS Continuum—the
Physical, Emotional, Mental and Spiritual levels of
experience.

It is essential to bring your ideals and aspirations
down into practical manifestation at the physical level.
This is exactly what the Essenes did two thousand years
ago: at that time they glimpsed the possibility of a New

World, a World aligned with the Light, and they worked with the angels to bring that Light into manifest reality upon the Earth. Focusing around two great teachers—Jeshua and Mary Magdalene—they set up a bold experiment, the attempt to understand and embody the All, which they approached through the energy of Unconditional Love working through the heart center:

Accepting all, you allow and nourish all.
Allowing all, you exclude none.
In this state, Love transcends the barriers
between you and me, greater and lesser,
past and present, possible and impossible.
Love simply IS, and it opens the door
not only to an understanding of the All
but to a way to live upon another level,
a level aligned directly with the Light.

Sadly, the Essene experiment could not be sustained, and for a time the Light passed out of human memory and human experience. But now, two thousand years later, another great opportunity to manifest the Light emerges. As your planet moves upwards in vibration, many human beings are experiencing a process of transformation and awakening. Once again there is closer contact with the angelic realm, and the angels are preparing to sing a new song:

We sing the freedom and joy
    of an Awakening Humanity.
We sing the Brotherhood/Sisterhood
    of angels and of human beings.
We sing the Transition of the Earth.
We sing the Triumph of the Light.

This is the High Magic, the magic of the Spirit, through which all hurts are healed, and all things are made new.

This is the opening of the door to a multidimensional experience as humanity awakens and your planet becomes a sacred planet within a galaxy that is returning to Source.

This is the beginning of a new life, in which the Children of the Light return from their wanderings and rise into the wonder of eternal joy.

Afterword:

A Kind of Magic

We are not accustomed to magic,
and the nearest we allow
a spell to enter our lives
is to look out upon a sunset,
or listen to a skilled musician.

We are not accustomed to magic,
and the very thought of it
sends a little shiver
down the modern spine.

We have squeezed magic out of our world,
explained it away in a logical fashion,
and consigned it to history.
The trouble is that it will not stay there,
and every now and then
it breaks out and confronts us
with a miracle.
Oh yes, they will explain it away
if you give them enough time,
but the fact remains
that we are spiritual beings,
and in the deepest corner of our consciousness
the Spirit weaves a kind of magic.

When the Spirit speaks,
the hardest heart cracks open to reveal
the core of love which was hiding there
all the time.

When the Spirit speaks,
the barriers dissolve
and peace breaks out against the odds.

When the Spirit speaks,
you don't need to reason
or understand any more,
for in a single moment *you know:*
and in that knowing rests healing and transformation
beyond your wildest dreams.

Epilogue 1:

The New Media

Many people are now exploring new levels of empowerment through using the new media, particularly social networking and internet radio.

Social networking links people in immediate and personal ways, supporting the democratization of knowledge and empowering individuals whatever the political environment.

Internet radio empowers Lightworkers by providing a vital resource of information on new ideas and the New Consciousness.

The importance of internet radio stations as a vital resource in a time of change is now being more widely recognized. The most effective format here is the one-hour weekly show in which the host can dialogue with guests who have interesting ideas to share about the changes that are happening in our lives. Add the efficiency of international phone cables connecting host with guests through optical fibre technology so that the host can be in America and the guests in UK, or Europe, or Australia, and you get a glimpse of the truly global nature of internet radio.

Listening live to these shows is only part of their appeal. There is also an archive of past shows which is a real treasure house of alternative information. Leading internet radio stations that offer a progressive and alternative view of the world include:

www.bbsradio.com
www.radiooutthere.com
www.soulsjourneyradio.com

www.worldpuja.org

Epilogue 2:

Foundation for Crystal Children

Our website (see the Feedback From Readers section) is given as "Foundation for Crystal Children," and we are getting emails from all over the world asking about this foundation. Our foundation is still in the earliest stages of its development. We are just beginning to build a network of parents of crystal children and of educators and therapists who wish to improve their knowledge of these new children, and we encourage anyone in these categories to contact us via the website.

The purpose of this network which we are starting to build is to put parents of crystal children in touch with one another, and to share information about the parenting, education, healing, and care of crystal children.

All this is in the earliest stages of development, so please be patient while the network builds. We have already had one query about possible funding to support parents of crystal children, but at this early stage in the network's development, no funding programs have been put in place.

Epilogue 3:

International Coordinators

One theme that has emerged strongly from many of the emails we get from readers is a need to contact and talk with like-minded people.

So many readers have asked us for contacts that we have set up a network of International Coordinators, one for each country (or group of countries) where we have readers. If you would like to contact other people in your area or in another country, please email your local Coordinator with your email address and the name of your country and nearest city. The Coordinator will then give you email addresses of any local readers who are on his/her list.

So far we have Coordinators in the following countries:

United Kingdom: Lyn and Graham Whiteman
    at essenes@btinternet.com

USA and Canada: Diane Richard at diane@biosophic.com

Australia: Jann Porter at rose.path@bigpond.com

Ireland: Christine Astell at c.angels@btinternet.com

Germany and Austria: Norbert and Karin
    Karin at bauschat.karin@web.de
    Norbert at beine.norbert@web.de

Netherlands and Belgium: ArjunA van Heerdt
    at info@assayya.com

Portugal: Martin Northey at martin.northey@mail.telepac.pt

Scandinavia: Anita Murray at anita.murray@ymail.com

Central Europe: To be agreed

Africa: Pieter van Nieuwenhuizen at pieter@sotiralis.co.za

Southeast Asia: To be agreed

Spain: Isabel Zaplana at i.zaplana@gematria.net

Bermuda: Mimi Harding at moomimi@logic.bm

France: To be agreed

If you would like to be a Coordinator for any country without a Coordinator or not listed, please contact us via our website—see the Feedback From Readers section.

Comment by Stuart: Please ask your coordinator about Gatherings in your area. In the UK the big Midsummer Essene Gathering is organized by the Essene Network International: please contact them through their website - www.essenenetwork.org   We now also have a Yahoo Group: to access this, go to www.groups.yahoo.com click on Yahoo Groups and enter essene_family in the Find a Group search box.

Atlantis and the New Consciousness

Further Reading

Andrews, Shirley (1999). *Atlantis: Insights from a lost civilization.* St. Paul, MN: Llewellyn. A useful summary of sources on Atlantis with a section summarizing Atlantean chronology.

Braden, Gregg (1997). *Awakening to zero point.* Bellvue, WA: Radio Bookstore Press. A helpful guide to the science underlying the transition of Earth and the change in consciousness.

Braden, Gregg, Russell, Peter, Stray, Geoff, and Jenkins, John (2008). *The mystery of 2012; Predictions,* prophecies and possibilities. Louisville, CO: Sounds True. Insightful essays by leading authors in this field. Recommended as one of the best general surveys of 2012.

Cooper, Diana, & Hutton, Shaaron (2005). *Discover Atlantis: A guide to reclaiming the wisdom of the* ancients. London: Hodder Mobius. An inspiring and informative introduction to the key era of Golden Atlantis.

Cooper, Diana (2005). *Atlantis Cards.* Forres, Scotland: Findhorn Press. A magical and inspiring set of cards illustrated by Damian Keenan.

Cooper, Diana (2009). *2012 and beyond: An invitation to meet the challenges and opportunities ahead* Forres, Scotland: Findhorn Press. A concise and helpful introduction to the significance of 2012 within the context of ancient prophecies and practical information to prepare for this time of change. Highly recommended.

French, Karen (2008). *Gateway to the heavens: How simple shapes mould reality and the fabric of your being.* ygb publishing, www.gatewaytotheheavens.com The best modern analysis of sacred geometry and its impact on life: simple, clear and easy to read.

Gawain,Shakti (1993). *The path of transformation: How healing ourselves can change the world.* Mill Valley, CA: Nataraj Publishing. Offers a clear understanding of the process of change, and practical ways to support it.

Holbeche, Soozi (1997). *Changes: A guide to personal transformation and new ways of living in the next millennium.* London: Piatkus. A book full of clarity and down-to-earth ideas to help us manage the process of change.

Hurtak, J. J. (1987). *The book of knowledge: The keys of Enoch.* Los Gatos, CA The Academy for Future Science. A profound and esoteric book which is widely regarded as the ultimate source-book on the metaphysical universe and the transformation of consciousness. www.keysofenoch.org

Merivale,Philippa (2009). *Rescued by angels.* Winchester: O-Books. The remarkable life-journey that led to the emergence of Metatronic Healing, a transformational system inspired by the great angel Metatron. (See www.metatronic-life.com)

Valee, Martine (Editor). (2009). *The great shift: Co-creating a new world for 2012 and beyond.* San Francisco, CA: Weiser Books. Some remarkable channeling by Lee Carroll, Tom Kenyon, and Patricia Cori.

Whitworth, Belinda (2005). *New age encyclopedia; A mind-body-spirit reference guide.* London: Robert Hale. An essential source book for any seeker in this time of transformation.

Wilson, Stuart and Prentis, Joanna (2009). *Power of the Magdalene*. Huntsville, AR: Ozark Mountain Publishing. This is our second book and contains a lot more information about the female disciples of Jeshua and a whole section on the New Children, especially the Crystal Children.

Wilson, Stuart and Prentis, Joanna (2010). *Beyond limitations: The Power of Conscious Co-creation*. Huntsville, AR: Ozark Mountain Publishing, Channeled information which reveals the link between reality creation and the 2012 experience. This is the first book to reveal all three levels of reality creation. It provides a complete answer to the question, "How do we create our own reality?"

Wilson, Stuart and Passmore, Sarah (n.d.). *Creating abundance*. Huntsville, AR: Ozark Mountain Publishing. A complete guide to manifesting a joyful and abundant life. Practical techniques for removing blocks, enhancing creativity, and achieving empowerment. Now in production with Ozark Mountain Publishing; Huntsville, AR

Wilson, Stuart (n.d.) *The Magdalene Version: Secret Wisdom from a Gnostic Mystery School*. Huntsville, AR: Ozark Mountain Publishing. Channeling from Alariel reveals eight Keynote Speeches given by Mary Magdalene during Midsummer Gatherings on the island of Cyprus.

Note: Some of the books cited above may be difficult to obtain from general bookshops; however, you can buy them from the following sites:

Arcturus Books: www.arcturusbooks.co.uk,
    phone 01803 864363;

Aristia: www.aristia.co.uk , phone 01983 721060;

Cygnus Books: www.cygnus-books.co.uk,
    phone 01550 777701.

Acknowledgments

We would like to say a big "thank you" to those whose past life experiences form the core of this book. Your input was essential, and there would have been no book without you.

> Catherine Mary La Toure
> Ken Driver

Our thanks to Diana Cooper and Shaaron Hutton for their inspiring book on Golden Atlantis. We heard Diana's talk at the Axminster Awareness Center just as we were starting a major cycle of past-life regression focusing on Atlantis. Thank you, Diana, for all your work and your perfect timing!

We are grateful to Belinda Whitworth and Bob Maddox for their advice regarding source-books on Atlantis. These proved useful during the research stage which followed the regression cycle.

We would like to say a big *thank you* to the whole Ozark Mountain Publishing team, especially Dolores Cannon, Julia Degan, Nancy Garrison, and Joy Newman. Thank you for helping us to get these new perspectives out into the world!

High Priestess 44, 102
Horus 55
Hurtak, J.J. 43
Hutton, Shaaron 39, 42

Indigo Children 118
Intergalactic Council 93-5, 100-2, 104
Interlife 120
Isreal v, 61

Jardine, Tatanya v
Jeshua 59-61, 125, 140, 145

Kayden, Atlantean poet 77-9
King, Gisele iv

La Toure, Catherine Mary 51, 53, 73, 119
Lemuria 62, 102, 105
Light Body 74, 140-1
lightness, principles of 134
Love, Unconditional 59-60, 63, 140, 142, 145-6

Magdalene, Mary 145
magic 123, 143, 146, 149
Markham, Ursula v
Mayan Calendar 111
meditational form of movement 17, 31-2
Melchizedek, Order of 32-3, 55
Merivale, Philippa 132
Metatronic Healing 133
Mitchell Hedges, Anna v
Mount Carmel 32

Native American 58, 83
New Consciousness 117, 137-144
New Testament vi
New World 89, 112, 119, 145

Om 85
Oneness 49, 93, 143-5
Orintha 65
Orion 58

Pele 62
PEMS Continuum 145
perfume 75
Phases of Atlantis 97-104
Priestess 42-3, 50, 58
pyramid 19, 41, 57-8

Rainbow Children 118, 138, 142
Reconnective Healing 43
Revolution in Consciousness 138
Roman era 61

St Germain 125
Sams, Jamie 84
Sirius 3-17, 54, 58
Sirius Grid 54
Solantha 8, 10, 11, 15
souls, group and human 103
sound 17
Source, the 50, 93, 111
spiral of human development 88
Spirit 81, 89, 116, 123, 143, 146, 150
star beings 93, 106, 116
star-wisdom 68
Starlight Centre v
starship crashes 3-8
sting-ray design 73
story and drama 80
Sykla 41

Tai Chi 31
Technology of Light 118, 140
telepathy 48
terra-forming 95
therapy techniques 24, 43
Tibet 85

Totality of Being 145
transformation, principles of 112,
    115-6
Transition of the Earth
    107, 116-7, 121-3, 126, 146

university 15

Wise Ones 100-102, 106

Yoga of the New Age 133

Zaplana, Isabel vi
Zaritha 23-7
Zoltha, Temple of 45
Zoroaster 59

About the Authors

Joanna Prentis: I was born in Bangalore in southern India. When I was nearly three, my family returned to Scotland where I spent my childhood and teenage years. After leaving school, I traveled extensively, married and lived in Hong Kong for two years and then ten years in the bush in Western Australia, where my three daughters were born. It was there that my interest began in alternative medicine and education, organic farming, metaphysics and meditation. With a local nurse, we ran a Homeopathic and Radionic practice.

I returned to the UK in 1979 and later trained as a Montessori teacher, educating my two youngest daughters, Katinka and Larissa, at home for a few years. I now have four beautiful grandchildren.

I did several healing courses and have a foundation diploma in Humanistic Psychology. I also trained with Ursula Markham and have a diploma in Hypnotherapy and Past Life Therapy.

With my eldest daughter Tatanya, I set up the Starlight Centre in 1988, a centre for healing and the expansion of consciousness. Over the years, Tatanya has introduced us to many innovative techniques and interesting people.

In 1999 we closed the Centre to focus on producing our books. I continue with my Past Life work, and readers now connect with us from all over the world.

You can visit Joanna at her website:
www.foundationforcrystalchildren.com

COPYRIGHT WYN PENNANT JONES PHOTOGRAPHIC ART

Stuart Wilson is a writer on new perspectives: His perceptions have been developed through 30 years of working with groups committed to personal growth. For nine years, Stuart co-focalized (with Joanna Prentis) the Starlight Centre in the West of England, a centre dedicated to healing and the transformation of consciousness.

He writes about this period:

"It was inspiring and fascinating but also exhausting! A stream of visitors came in to the Centre, mainly from the United States and Australia, but some also from Europe. We had an amazing and mind-bending time sitting at the feet of internationally respected spiritual teachers and workshop leaders."

Part of the work of the Centre was research into past lives, and this led to his collaboration with Joanna to write *The Essenes, Children of the Light* and *Power of the Magdalene*, both published by Ozark Mountain Publishing

You can visit Stuart at his website:
www.foundationforcrystalchildren.com

Feedback from Readers

Please let us know what you feel about this book: you can contact us through our website:

www.foundationforcrystal children.com

We are sometimes asked by readers when the next Starlight Centre meeting will be. Although the Starlight Centre doesn't meet physically any more (as we're now focusing on producing books), we do "meet" on our website and through our growing email correspondence with readers all over the world. And if you're visiting the West of England and want to come and see us, please email because we both have a busy schedule.

Alariel does not do individual or group channeling sessions. All our dialogues with him are focused on producing these books. However, we are open to receiving questions from readers. Just email them to us and we will put them to Alariel at an appropriate time. Please bear in mind that Alariel does not take personal questions, or make predictions about the future of individuals or groups.

Other Books by
Stuart Wilson and Joanna Prentis

The Essenes, Children of the Light

The inner story of the Essene Brotherhood, seen from the past life perspective of Daniel, an Essene elder, and his friend Joseph of Arimathea. Tells the dramatic story of Jesus' healing in the tomb and reveals Essene links with the Druids and the Order of Melchizedek.

Power of the Magdalene

A blend of the past life experiences of seven subjects and channeling by Alariel. Reveals the existence of a group of female disciples, and the real significance of Mary Magdalene as the spiritual partner of Jeshua. Contains a whole section on the New Children who are now being born.

Beyond Limitations: The Power of Conscious Co-Creation

Channeled information from the angelic source Alariel which provides a complete answer to the question, "How do we create our own reality?" A revolutionary text which reveals the connection between reality creation and the 2012 experience. This is quite simply the most advanced book on reality creation available anywhere.

Also by Stuart Wilson:
Creating Abundance by Stuart Wilson and Sarah Passmore

A complete guide to manifesting a joyful and abundant life. Practical techniques for removing blocks, enhancing creativity and achieving empowerment. Now in production with Ozark Mountain Publishing. For date of publication, please see their website: www.ozarkmt.com

The Magdalene Version: Secret Wisdom from a Gnostic Mystery School by Stuart Wilson

Channeling which reveals the secret teachings which Mary Magdalene gave in her Mystery School. These teachings show a profound understanding of the Way which Jeshua taught. Now in production with Ozark Mountain Publishing. For date of publication, please see their website: www.ozarkmt.com

Other Books Published
by
Ozark Mountain Publishing, Inc.

Continue for more books by Ozark Mountain Publishing, Inc.

For more information about any of the above titles, soon to be released titles, or
other items in our catalog, write or visit our website:

OZARK
MOUNTAIN
PUBLISHING

PO Box 754
Huntsville, AR 72740
www.ozarkmt.com
1-800-935-0045/479-738-2348
Wholesale Inquiries Welcome